WARSHIPS

WARSHIPS

NORMAN POLMAR
and
NORMAN FRIEDMAN

Sundial

Dedication
For Beverly and Rhea
and their patience

First published in Great Britain in 1981 by
Octopus Books Limited
59 Grosvenor Street London W1

© 1981 Hennerwood Publications Limited

ISBN 0 906320 07 0

Produced by Mandarin Publishers Limited
22a Westlands Road Quarry Bay Hong Kong

Printed in Hong Kong

Endpapers HMS *Alacrity*, one of the *Amazon*-class
(Type 21) frigates, which entered service in 1971.
Half-title page: HMS *Warrior* (1860), the world's
first iron-hulled warship.
Title page: HMS *Invincible*, one of the through-
deck anti-submarine cruisers.
This page: USS *New Jersey* (57,540 tons) escorts
the *Essex*-class carrier *Intrepid* in the western Pacific
during World War II.

CONTENTS

CHAPTER 1
INNOVATION

Nelson's flagship at Trafalgar, the three-deck ship-of-the-line *Victory* (2,162 tons), had an overall length of about 69 m (226 ft). Her armament included thirty 32-pounder guns on her lower gun deck, twenty-eight 24-pounders on her middle deck, and thirty 12-pounders on her upper deck; also mounted were twelve 12-pounders and two 68-pounder carronades.

It is about 200 years since the beginning of the Industrial Revolution foreshadowed the transformation of the world's navies from wooden-hulled, sail-powered vessels to the iron and steel, mechanically powered ships of the 19th and 20th centuries.

The Industrial Revolution began a cycle of more and more rapid change, so that ships and even whole technologies now last little more than two decades, whereas at one time the working life of a ship was limited only by its physical endurance. The ship-of-the-line *Victory* was regarded as a modern battleship when she served as Horatio Nelson's flagship at Trafalgar in 1805. Yet she had been launched 40 years before and she represented a naval technology that had changed little since the mid-15th century. Moreover, HMS *Victory* continued to be an effective capital ship until as late as the 1840s. One warship could thus exemplify a technological period of some 400 years. By way of contrast, very few warships built at the end of World War II, only 35 years ago, continue in service in any major navy; moreover, many which do remain have been so thoroughly rebuilt as to be virtually new ships.

This accelerating revolution of naval technology is really three revolutions. First there was the revolution of steam power and of iron- and steel-making, which brought, first, steam engines in place of sail, then shell-firing guns and, as a consequence, protective armour, and then stronger metal hulls which permitted larger and larger ships to be built. Still later the steam turbine greatly increased ship speed and endurance, and made possible naval war over vast distances.

Late in the 19th century came the second revolution, that of the internal-combustion engine. This made possible the submarine, the aeroplane, and the motor torpedo boat. In some ways, the torpedo was also an early product of this revolution. Later products include the gas-turbine, or turbojet, engine that propels many modern warships.

Later still came the third revolution: electronics. It brought, first, radio, which allowed communication between widely dispersed ships. Then came underwater listening devices (the forerunners of asdic and sonar), followed by radar, computers and, most recently, guided anti-aircraft and anti-ship missiles.

H.M.S. AGINCOURT,
IRON-CLAD 28 GUNS.
Flag Ship of the Western Division of the Channel Squadron
Published by H. M. Currie, 79, Union St. Stonehouse Devon.

Among the earliest British warships to have an iron hull was the armoured frigate *Agincourt* of 1865. Of 10,700 tons and 122 m (400 ft) long, she and her two sisters were the only five-masters in the battle fleet. Her hull armour was reinforced by a backing of teak 254 mm (10 in) thick, and her main armament was four 229 mm (9 in) muzzle-loading guns.

The Coming of Steam

The first naval fruit of the Industrial Revolution, then, was steam power: no longer would ships be entirely at the mercy of the wind. There were, however, drawbacks, which rather slowed the adoption of this form of power. For example, early steam engines were voracious consumers of fuel, so that a warship entirely dependent upon steam power would have a very short cruising range. In contrast, sailing warships had, in effect, unlimited range – a happy state which would not recur until the advent of nuclear power.

Even today, navies have no equivalent of the freedom from bases which the sailing navies knew. In Nelson's day a squadron of warships could cruise for perhaps three years without returning to its base. The ships could put in at isolated bays to 'refit', using spare sails and other stores carried on board, and local timber if repairs were needed. Food supplies could be bought (or captured) ashore every few months, and water barrels could be filled at any isolated stream near a coast.

For the major navies concerned with keeping the peace in distant seas, the need for fuelling stations was a serious disadvantage of steam power, and it is the main reason why warships combined sails and steam until quite late in the 19th century during much of this period steam was used mainly for manoeuvring, especially in harbour and in action, while sail was used for cruising in order to conserve fuel. Steam also received a reluctant naval welcome because it made for a dirty ship: during coaling the dust would cover a ship's gleaming wooden deck and white or light-grey super-structure, and would even penetrate the cabins and other below-deck areas.

In the early days of steam power there was a third and even more serious problem. The first steamships were propelled by paddle wheels – huge wheels, mounted along the side of the hull, that not only took up a large portion of the broadside that would otherwise be devoted to cannon, but presented a fragile and almost unmissable target for an enemy's guns. Large-scale use of steam in warships had to await the invention of the screw propeller, which was wholly under water and so invulnerable to shellfire and, moreover, took up no broadside space. By the 1850s, new ships were beginning to be built with propellers, and many older ones, including battleships (that is, line-of-battle ships), were being converted.

Armour

The Crimean War of 1854 showed just how valuable the propeller could be for manoeuvring in confined spaces under adverse wind conditions. The war also led to another great naval innovation of the 19th century – the use of armour. Well before the war, guns firing explosive shells instead of cannonballs had been developed and introduced into several navies. Like many other military innovations, this one was not sufficiently appreciated at the time. In fact, the explosive shell doomed the wooden warship. Wood was an excellent shipbuilding material as long as guns fired solid shot, which simply punched holes in ships and cut rigging: it was possible to patch a wooden hull, even in battle. Explosive shells, on the other hand, were capable of tearing wooden ships apart or setting them on fire.

Hitherto, navies had rejected the use of iron because experiments had shown iron hulls to be dangerously brittle. The introduction of explosive shells, however, enforced the development of armoured vessels in which timber hulls were strengthened by encasing them in iron plate (whence the term 'ironclad' that was used to describe many 19th-century warships). Armoured sea-going warships were built first in France and Britain, then in the United States and in other countries.

From about 1860 onward naval officers struggled to understand the implications of steam and armour. Wooden warships were restricted in the size of the guns they could carry by the strength of their structures and of the men who had to man-handle the weapons and ammunition. A wooden warship was classified by the number of guns she carried. HMS *Victory*, one of the larger ships-of-the-line of her day, had 102 cannon of various sizes on three decks, plus two carronades (stubby giants for action at close quarters).

The coming of armour changed all that. Ships carried far fewer guns – first, because guns capable of piercing armour had to be much larger and heavier; and, second, because the weight of their own protective armour had to be balanced by some reduction in other weights, particularly in weights high in a ship. The first British armoured battleship, HMS *Warrior*, launched in 1860, had a single gun deck with 40 guns and was powered by both steam and sail. As the quality of armour plating improved, ever larger and more powerful guns had to be fitted; these, too, had to be protected by armour, which added still further to their weight. To make them easier to handle and aim, the largest guns were mounted on turntables. The first ship to be fitted with an armoured revolving gun turret was the U.S. Navy's ironclad *Monitor* of 1862. Within two decades the armoured revolving turret was almost universal in large warships, and the biggest guns were loaded and turned mechanically, using steam power from the engines.

Between 1860 and 1880 the contest between the destructive power of naval guns and the protective capacity of armour was generally in favour of the latter: the iron and steel founders usually managed to keep a couple of steps ahead if the gun makers. Some naval leaders even predicted the end of gun duels at sea and began to look for new types of offensive weapon.

Among a number of bizarre ideas put forward about this time was the installation of a ram, built into the underwater bow of a ship, that would be used to pierce the hull of an enemy vessel. Although employed with surprising success at the Battle of Lissa in 1866, the ram was totally anachronistic – a throwback to the war gallies of classical times.

Although, in theory, the principal task of navies of the 19th century was to fight a new Battle of Trafalgar, in fact most of their work did not call for the use of the impressive new armoured ships. For instance, the Royal Navy served largely as a kind of maritime police force during this period, and for such duty it required large numbers of warships powerful enough to beat down pirate vessels preying upon merchantmen and impressive enough to deter colonial peoples from causing trouble in the outposts of empire. Because many were needed, these ships had to be comparatively cheap to build and operate. In contrast to the leviathans of the battle fleet, such long-range 'cruisers' were relatively small and, in form and function, little different from their sailing frigate ancestors. They were, to be sure, steam-powered, but cruising on distant stations demanded good sailing qualities because coal was not always available and was, moreover, expensive.

As the great-power rivalry for colonies intensified in the latter half of the century, however, even ships destined for cruising in distant waters were affected by the revolution in naval technology. By the 1880s such ships were fitted with deck (though not yet with side) armour, and these 'protected cruisers' were armed with modern guns and with the newly developed torpedoes.

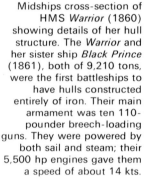

Midships cross-section of HMS *Warrior* (1860) showing details of her hull structure. The *Warrior* and her sister ship *Black Prince* (1861), both of 9,210 tons, were the first battleships to have hulls constructed entirely of iron. Their main armament was ten 110-pounder breech-loading guns. They were powered by both sail and steam; their 5,500 hp engines gave them a speed of about 14 kts.

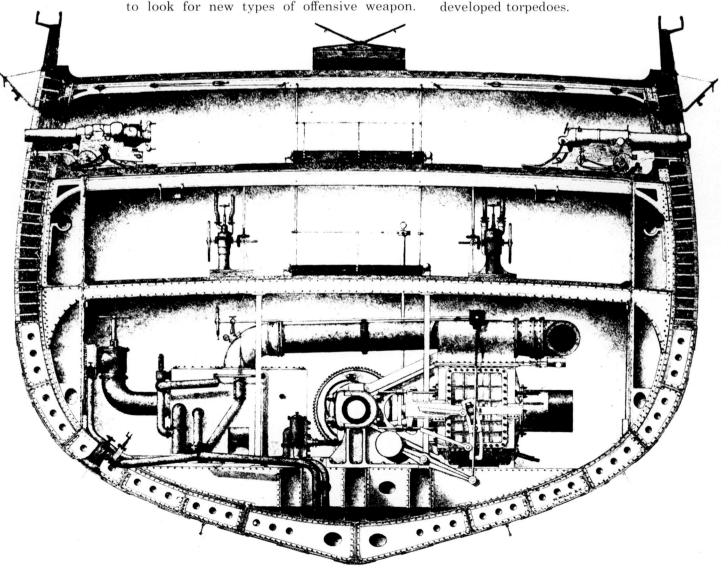

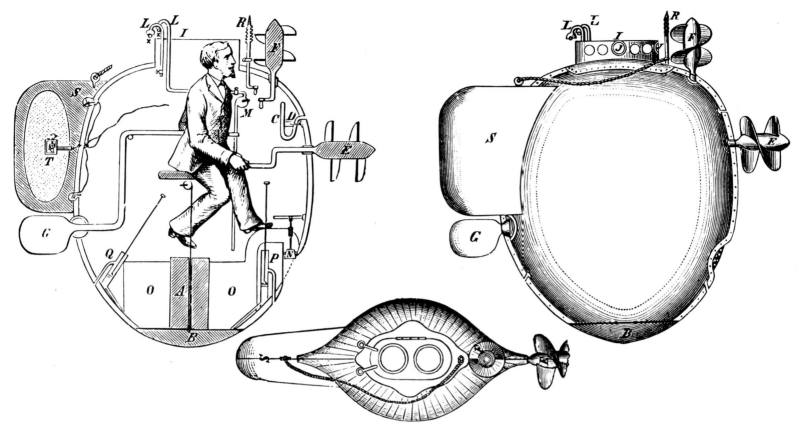

Underwater Explosives

The technological revolution and international rivalry enormously increased the cost of sea power. Whereas in the 17th and 18th centuries the maritime nations of Denmark and Sweden had operated large battle fleets, neither could afford to build a battle fleet of armoured, steam-powered warships in the 19th, and by the end of the century their navies had been reduced mainly to coastal-defence ships. This rising cost inspired a long series of attempts to circumvent the mainstream of naval development – to find some inexpensive method of destroying the large and impressive battleships. Even before the dawn of the steam age, some had seen an answer in the use of underwater explosives. During the American War of Independence (1776) David Bushnell planned an attack on the British warship HMS *Eagle* in New York harbour, using a primitive submarine and explosive kegs which the operator, an army sergeant named Ezra Lee, tried to attach to the enemy's hull. Lee's efforts were frustrated because the wooden hull of the British ship was sheathed with copper to protect it from marine organisms, and the devices for attaching the explosives would not penetrate the sheathing.

During the Napoleonic Wars the American Robert Fulton (1765–1815), a pioneer of maritime steampower, offered a more advanced submarine to both England and France. The Royal Navy rejected his proposal, partly on the ground that if it did make conventional battle fleets obsolete Britain, with by far the most powerful such fleet in the world, would be the principal loser. Underwater explosives, anchored to the seabed in harbours or other shallow waters, remained through the 19th century the weapon of the weaker navies as a counter against blockade. They were used extensively and very successfully in the American Civil War (1861–5), but did not really come to maturity until they were married to a means of self-propulsion,

initially in the 'automobile' torpedo designed jointly by the Scottish engineer Robert Whitehead and Captain Giovanni de Luppis, formerly of the Austrian Navy.

The torpedo promised something quite new: a weak power, or one preferring to spend its resources on land warfare, could commission a large number of small torpedo boats manned by heroes who would willingly go out to destroy the large and expensive capital ships of the enemy. Weapon begets counter-weapon, however, and the torpedo boats of the late 1800s were soon confronted by small-calibre, quick-firing guns installed in battleships and then in specially designed 'torpedo-boat destroyers.' These destroyers were larger than their prey and exceptionally fast. (Later, they would also be armed with torpedoes and become dual-purpose ships.) As it turned out, the battleship-sinking potential of the early torpedo boats was never realised, for the small craft were not sufficiently seaworthy to take on capital ships in open waters.

The naval revolution of the 19th century took place in a vacuum: apart from the Battle of Lissa (1866) there was no full-scale engagement on the high seas between the battle fleets of the major powers during this period. Five generations of battleships went from builder to breaker having fired scarcely a shot in anger, so that there were few opportunities for the great powers to put new technology to the acid test.

That is not to say that the 19th century offered no practical pointers to the future of naval warfare. There were, indeed, many engagements that, although mostly small in scale, were studied avidly by the admiralties of the great powers. As we shall see in the next chapter, the conclusions drawn from such studies were not always sound, but they form an important backcloth to the prodigious naval build-up in Europe in the closing years of the century.

David Bushnell's one-man submersible *Turtle* of 1776. Horizontal and vertical movements were by means of hand-turned helical screws (E, F). The vessel submerged when water flooded the reservoirs (O) via a foot-operated valve (N), and surfaced when the water was expelled by pumps (P, Q). The 68 kg (150 lb) mine (S) was roped to a screw drill (R), by which it could be attached to an enemy hull.

CHAPTER 2
TRIAL BY FIRE

The long peace of the 19th century was broken by several wars at a time when the naval revolution was beginning to gain momentum. On 20 November 1853 the Russian Vice-Admiral Povel Nakhimov led five ships-of-the-line through rain and fog into the Turkish Black Sea port of Sinope (Sinop). His main batteries, consisting of guns firing 31 kg (68 lb) explosive shells, sank all seven Turkish frigates in the port, silenced the shore batteries, and set fire to the town. The Russians won a crushing victory and killed almost 3,000 Turks.

In the Crimean War that followed (1854–6) Turkey's allies, Britain and France, moved fleets into the Baltic and Black seas with the object of seizing the main Russian fleet bases at Kronshtadt and Sevastopol, respectively. In both cases they learnt to their cost that their fleets, built for high-seas engagements, were not suited to a war in which the Russians withdrew their ships and fought with powerful shore batteries. The battleships of both Allied navies drew far too much water to come close enough to bear their guns on the Russian forts, and most of them were sail-powered and could not manoeuvre effectively inshore.

The pounding sustained by the British and French ships demonstrated with terrible clarity the need for fighting vessels to be protected with armour. Recent British and French experience in building large, armoured, floating gun batteries could not be translated directly into battleship construction because such batteries had to have a very shallow draught and therefore offered very poor seagoing performance. Moreover, although the batteries were self-propelled, there was no need for them to be particularly fast or manoeuvrable – two qualities essential in a battleship. However, the advance they represented seemed to the French to offer an opportunity to achieve naval supremacy. Some French naval leaders felt that, with the construction of an armoured battleship, the entire expensive British battle fleet would become obsolete. The French did indeed launch the world's first armoured seagoing warship, the *Gloire* (1858), which had iron plates fitted over a wooden hull and displaced 5,617 tons. But Britain, with her more capable shipbuilding industry, soon overcame the French lead. In fact, Britain's first armoured warship, the 9,210-ton *Warrior* (1860), whose hull still exists, was the first warship to have an iron rather than a wooden hull. This was a significant step forward: iron hulls are far stronger than wooden ones. They not only were better able to take the weights of, and stresses imposed by, the new, very heavy armour-piercing guns; they also allowed the construction of far larger ships than ever before.

Below The French *Gloire*
(1858) was the first warship
to have a wooden hull
protected by iron plating
along most of its length.
Anglo-French naval rivalry
was intense in the mid-19th
century, and the *Gloire*'s
innovation inspired the
construction of HMS *Warrior*.

The American Civil War

Neither the *Warrior* nor the *Gloire* ever saw action. However, just as they were being completed, the American Civil War (1861–5) began across the Atlantic. At its outbreak the Union (Northern) Navy consisted of a conventional collection of steam- and sail-powered frigates – which had, however, been scattered around the world on the orders of the Secretary of the Navy, who supported the Confederate (Southern) cause. The Confederate Navy was virtually non-existent and, moreover, the South had very little in the way of an industrial or shipbuilding base. What it did have was great determination and ingenuity – and the shattered remains of the Norfolk Navy Yard in Virginia. At Norfolk was the large steam frigate *Merrimack*, which the Union forces had burned and scuttled.

The Confederates realized at once that they could not hope to match the numerical strength of the Union Navy, and they resolved upon a dual policy: denial of Southern rivers to invading Union forces, and world-wide privateer warfare by cruisers, many of which were bought and equipped by sympathisers in Europe. For its part, the Union declared a naval blockade of the South, hoping to starve it of munitions and manufactured goods and at the same time to deny it the opportunity to raise capital abroad through the export of cotton, its chief cash crop. The effort at blockade ultimately included attempts to seize most Southern harbours, and in the west it included river war on a scale not seen again for 100 years.

The Confederate Navy saw in the new technology its chance to overcome the Northern lead in industry and numbers. The *Merrimack* was salvaged. She was not worth refitting as a frigate and she was never again really seaworthy, but she was strengthened by massive oak beams and planking overlain on her superstructure by 102 mm (4 in) iron plate. She was armed with 10 guns, including three smoothbores of 230 mm (9 in) calibre. Renamed the css *Virginia*, she dominated Hampton Roads, at the southern end of Chesapeake Bay, in March 1862 destroying two Union warships in her first action by ramming them with her specially strengthened bow and by gunfire.

The threat of the *Virginia* was soon answered by the Union's *Monitor*, designed by John Ericsson (who had pioneered the design of screw propellers in 1839). The *Monitor*, displacing 1,225 tons, had a flat deck almost flush with the waterline, and its hull was clad in 127 mm (5 in) iron plate. Its armament consisted of two 280 mm (11 in) smooth-bore guns mounted within an armoured turret rotated by its own steam engine.

The *Monitor* was towed south from her New York shipyard and arrived at Hampton Roads the day after the *Virginia*'s triumph. There followed the first-ever duel between ironclads. It proved inconclusive. Not even the 75 kg (166 lb) shot of the *Monitor*'s guns could penetrate the primitive armour of her adversary, although their impacts caused considerable minor damage; nor was either vessel handy enough to ram her opponent, although each tried several times. Even so, the presence of the *Monitor* in these waters ended the *Virginia*'s supremacy.

After the battle the *Virginia* withdrew up the James river, and later was blown up to prevent her capture by Union troops. As for the *Monitor*, her unseaworthiness doomed her, and she foundered off the mouth of Chesapeake Bay while under tow. However, the *Monitor*'s success inspired the construction of 21 more turret ships, which were classified as monitors; a few were even intended for ocean-going service, although these were never completed. The South, meanwhile, built a number of *Virginia*-type floating batteries. They were involved in several battles with the *Monitor*'s successors; none was sunk by the Union ships, although most were eventually forced to surrender after their crews had taken a terrible pounding from the monitors' shot.

The Confederacy also tried several unconventional weapons. Harbours and rivers were mined to restrict Union water-borne activities. In many cases these mines (at that time often known as 'torpedoes') could be exploded by electrical signals carried through cables from observation posts on shore. During the four-year Civil War more vessels were sunk by Confederate mines than by any other weapon – a total of 31 Union ships, including a monitor.

The *Monitor* and *Virginia* at close quarters in the Battle of Hampton Roads in 1862 – the first-ever engagement between ironclads.

The Confederate Navy also used 'mobile' mines in the form of spar torpedoes – explosive devices attached to booms protruding from the prows of small craft, some of which were semi-submersible. Such craft can be regarded as the ancestors of the motor torpedo boat. The Confederates also used primitive submarines, with hand-crank propulsion, fitted with spar torpedoes or mines towed behind them, the object being to drag the explosive devices against the enemy's ships. One such craft, the *H.L. Hunley*, fashioned from a 12 m (40 ft) iron boiler and with a crew of eight, made what may have been history's first successful submarine attack. On the night of 17 February 1864 the craft sank the Union steam frigate *Housatonic* outside the harbour of Charleston, South Carolina. The mine detonated the frigate's magazines – but the wave from the explosion swamped the *Hunley* and her entire crew drowned.

Another naval development of the Civil War was the Confederate attempt to cripple the Union economy through the destruction of its large merchant marine by commerce raiders. Eighteen cruisers, notably the *Alabama*, *Shenandoah*, and *Florida*, sank or captured more than 200 Union merchantmen. Although their success failed to defeat the North (and, incidentally, left the United States with virtually no merchant fleet at the end of the war), it led to a development that was to influence naval construction in Europe. The Union Navy had no counter to the commerce raiders' sudden and quite unpredictable attacks on merchant ships, which often took place hundreds, even thousands, of miles from American waters. There was no radio communication in those days, so that news about attacks had to await the arrival of survivors at Union ports. In view of such delays, the Union Navy decided to build a number of exceptionally fast cruisers to hunt down the commerce raiders. In the event, these ships were not completed until the war was over, but one of them, the USS *Wampanoag*, launched in 1867, established a world steamship record of $17\frac{3}{4}$ knots. The *Wampanoag* inspired the construction of several British cruisers of similar size and speed, and rather more heavily armed (she herself had sacrificed armament and even hull strength to achieve her speed, and consequently was ill-suited to any save her specialized wartime duty). The *Wampanoag* is a good example of the conflict between technology and conservatism in navies. She was a fine example of steam engineering, but at the end of the Civil War the U.S. Navy's principal concern on the high seas was the protection of American commerce in distant waters, where the capacity to remain on station for months on end was more important than high speed.

European naval observers of the American Civil War saw relatively little of relevance to their own problems. The U.S. Navy's monitors were clearly not capable of oceanic operation, although they might well be useful as coastal-defence craft. The war had offered no clue as to how ocean-going armoured ships would stand up in combat, particularly against the new generations of guns and armour-piercing shells that were being developed in Europe. River warfare seemed totally irrelevant, and it appears that whatever lessons the Confederate cruisers had taught regarding the protection of merchant ships were not taken to heart. The Union Navy had not the resources necessary to convoy its merchant ships, and in any case the Confederates had attacked in places where convoys were not practical.

The Union sloop *Kearsage* sinks the *Alabama*, one of the Confederate navy's most famous commerce raiders, in a battle off the French coast near Cherbourg in 1864.

17

The Battle of Lissa

In Europe, Austria and Italy came to blows in 1866, Italy being allied to Prussia in the latter's mainly land war with Austria. Their fleets met on 20 July in the Adriatic off the island of Lissa (now the Yugoslav Vis) in the first ironclad high-seas battle in history. Neither navy was well prepared for war. The Austrian flagship, for example, was to have been armed with new Krupp heavy guns, but these were embargoed, so she had to go to sea with obsolete weapons. The Italian flagship, the turret ship *Affondatore*, was not entirely complete, having just been delivered from a British yard. Only the Italian ships had rams, although the Austrian ironclads were reinforced at the bows by armour plating. At all events the Austrian commander, Admiral Wilhelm von Tegetthoff, ordered his ships to ram if the opportunity occurred. (It appears that the Italians did not share his views: presented with an Austrian ship broadside and dead in the water, one of the Italian captains, Count Faa di Bruno, refused to ram.) At the climax of the battle the Austrian flagship *Erzherzog Ferdinand Max* sank the 36-gun ironclad *Re d'Italia* by ramming her.

This dramatic success instantly re-established the ram as an essential weapon for ironclads. In retrospect, such a judgment is difficult to justify except on the assumption that armour would be immune to penetration by guns. In fact, given the armour-piercing shells that were being developed at the time, a ship attempting to ram would have been blown apart long before she could make contact. Indeed,

after Lissa, the ram proved more dangerous to friend than to foe: in 1893 the British battleship *Camperdown* accidentally rammed and sank HMS *Victoria*, the flagship of the Mediterranean Fleet. (A near-victim by drowning was one of *Victoria*'s junior officers, John Jellicoe, who was to be Commander-in-Chief of the Grand Fleet at the Battle of Jutland in 1916.)

Early Torpedoes

After Lissa, major European battle fleets were not to see action against each other until World War I. Whatever lessons were to be learnt had to come from the analysis of relatively small wars or individual engagements, in which a single armoured ship could have enormous influence. Among the most notable of these was the British-built ironclad monitor *Huascar*, which was bought by the Peruvian Navy in 1865. Although quite a small turret ship, she was for many years the most powerful warship in the Pacific Ocean. When her crew mutinied and turned pirate in 1877, all the Royal Navy could immediately oppose her with was a pair of large unarmoured frigates; no other navy in South America could provide even that much force. Neither British cruiser had weapons capable of penetrating the *Huascar's* armour, although both tried. For her part, the *Huascar's* gunnery was not up to destroying her two pursuers. The action is memorable because it was the first occasion on which a self-propelled Whitehead torpedo was fired in anger. This was, however, one of the early versions of the weapon, capable of only about nine knots, and it could not catch its target. The *Huascar* lived, to be captured by Chile in the 1879 War of the Pacific; she survives to this day.

Meanwhile, in 1878 the first successful torpedo attack had been made on the other side of the world, during the Russo-Turkish war. Whitehead had improved his torpedo, trebling its explosive power and doubling its speed to 18 knots, and one of them, launched at a range of 80 m, sank a Turkish warship in the Black Sea port of Batumi.

As for the great European battle fleets, built up at great cost, their operations were limited to manoeuvres to test the new technology and to naval demonstrations against colonial peoples, such as the French expedition to Indo-China in 1884 and the British naval bombardment of the Egyptian port of Alexandria in 1882. The interest of admiralties and naval theorists in such skirmishes reflects the dearth of practical experience in a time of rapidly changing ships and weapons. None of the experts in any of the great European navies knew what the future held in terms of wars at sea, and a host of different types of battleships, cruisers, destroyers, and other vessels was put into service. Indeed, in the 1870s the French Navy was known as the 'fleet of samples,' as all its capital ships differed from each other; some, burdened with change after change during construction, took as much as a decade from keel-laying to commissioning. In the United States the navy had been allowed to decay since the end of the Civil War. Calls to rebuild it foundered on conflicting views as to what kind of fleet was required, and it had to endure a long period of stagnation.

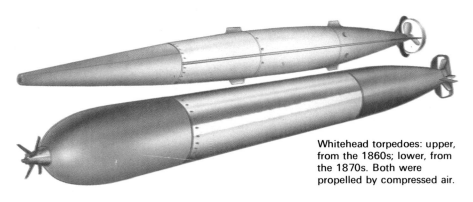

Whitehead torpedoes: upper, from the 1860s; lower, from the 1870s. Both were propelled by compressed air.

Above HMS *Inflexible* (1876), the first British battleship to have two turrets mounted *en echelon* amidships. Each had two 406 mm (16 in) muzzle-loading guns. The hull below the central citadel had 610 mm (24 in) armour plating backed by a belt of 432 mm (17 in) thick teak.

Left The iron frigate HMS *Shah* engages the pirate Peruvian armoured turret ship *Huascar* in 1877. This was the first action in which a Whitehead torpedo was used. It was, however, capable of only 9 kts, and the *Huascar* evaded it without difficulty.

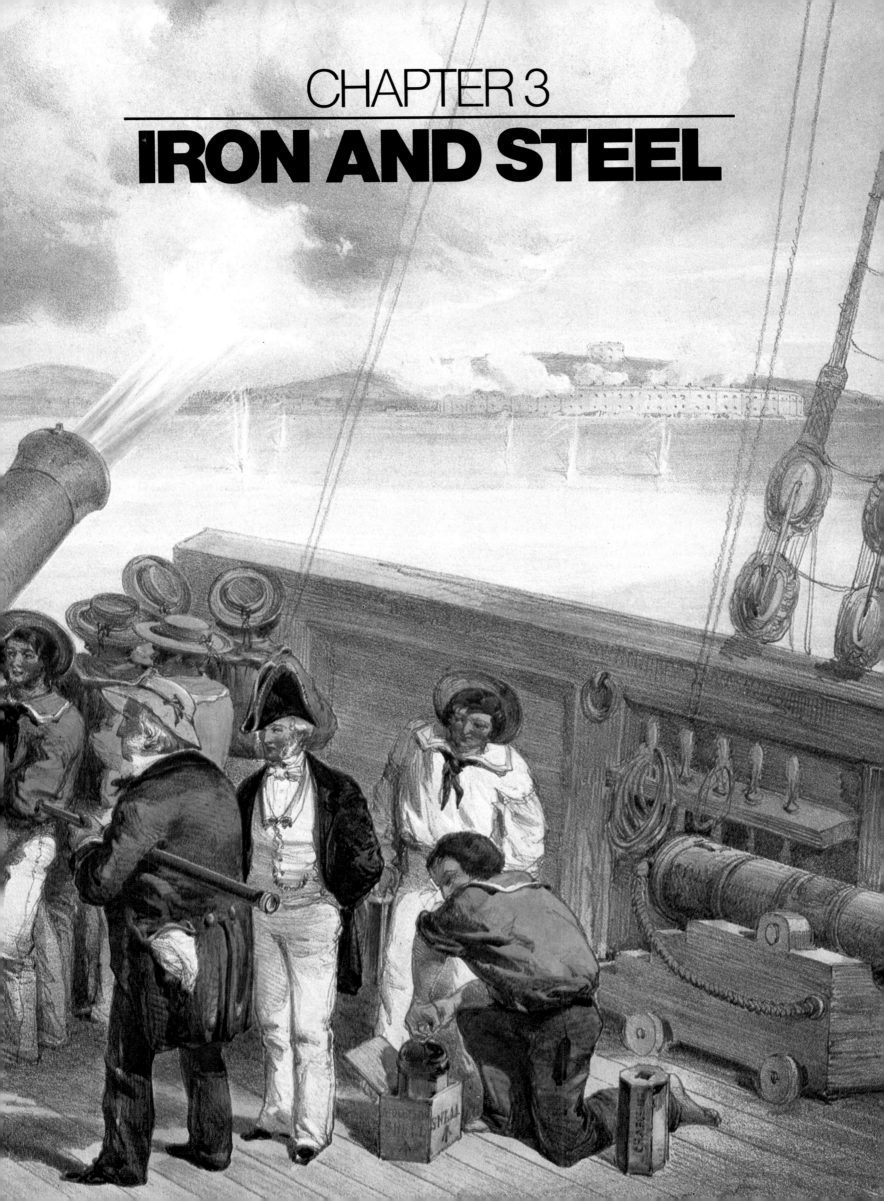

CHAPTER 3
IRON AND STEEL

Preceding two pages
HMS *Bulldog* bombarding
Russian shore batteries in the
Gulf of Finland in 1854.

The second half of the 19th century was marked by several notable advances in naval technology. In the absence of an opportunity to test them in war, however, these advances were not always efficiently exploited. For example, the main-battery guns of battleships increased steadily in internal diameter of barrel and in calibre (length of barrel), but they were rarely put to the test in target practice, which would have shown them to be wildly inaccurate at the sort of range at which they were intended to be used in battle. The shells and fuse mechanisms were also notoriously unreliable. In the British bombardment of Alexandria in 1882, a shell had landed harmlessly in the middle of 300 tons of gunpowder! Indeed, the biggest guns often seemed a greater danger to the ships in which they were installed than to an enemy. The largest Royal Navy gun of the 19th century, a 413 mm (16.25 in) weapon weighing 110 tons, produced so powerful a blast and so violent a recoil that it was seldom used in target practice for fear of damaging the ship's structure.

The Guns Evolve

The major developments in heavy guns were, first, breech-loading, and, second, slow-burning powder for high velocity. As guns became larger and more powerful, muzzle-loading – that is, loading the charge and then the shell at the mouth of the barrel, as with the old cannon – became more and more cumbersome, and as early as the 1860s breech-loaders were introduced into most navies. Breech-loading made it easier to rifle a gun. Rifling – lining the internal surface of the barrel with a spiral groove – imparts spin to a shell as it travels down the bore, and this greatly increases both its range and its accuracy. Rifling was essential for the longer shells that were the most effective for piercing armour. The development of ever-larger guns meant that ever-more-powerful charges were needed to propel the huge shells.

The breech, whether cast as part of the gun (as in a muzzle-loader) or separately (as in a breech-loader), had to be strong enough to withstand the violent explosion of the charge, so that the power of the expanding gases was directed solely toward propelling the shell. Early breeches were usually strong enough but care had to be taken to close them correctly. This was not always easy to verify, and in the 1870s, after several particularly bad accidents, the Royal Navy reverted for a time to muzzle-loaders. In the big muzzle-loaders, rifling was retained and the projectile, machined to match the rifling, was loaded by being very slowly 'screwed' into position atop its charge.

To modern eyes both muzzle- and breech-loaders of the 1870s and 1880s seem rather short. The reason is that they used a very quick-burning powder, all of whose energy was expended very rapidly in a short, sharp 'kick'. One disadvantage of this kind of kick was that it had a habit of detonating the explosive within the shell, with unfortunate results. The problem became so serious that an American proposed doing away with powder entirely, replacing it with compressed air, which would eject a 'dynamite torpedo' smoothly and efficiently. His arguments were cogent enough to persuade the U.S. Navy to build a 'dynamite cruiser,' the USS *Vesuvius*; but by the time she was ready slower-burning powders had largely solved the problem. Slower-burning powder required a longer barrel, so that the powder would have time to transfer its full energy to the projectile.

All the very heavy guns of the 19th century had a very slow rate of fire, in many cases not more than one shell every four or five minutes. Most large naval guns could be re-loaded only in one position, so that they had to be swung round, away from the target, brought to loading elevation, and loaded first with the shell and then with several bags of powder, before being swung back and re-sighted. Moreover, although

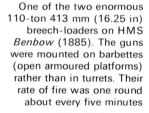

One of the two enormous
110-ton 413 mm (16.25 in)
breech-loaders on HMS
Benbow (1885). The guns
were mounted on barbettes
(open armoured platforms)
rather than in turrets. Their
rate of fire was one round
about every five minutes

such weapons had a theoretical range of perhaps 10,000 m (6.2 miles), they were inaccurate beyond about 2,000, a range at which much smaller weapons were also effective. By the 1880s the destructive power of the heaviest guns at such a short range could be countered only by armour so thick that even large ships could be clad with it only on limited sections of the hull, leaving large areas entirely unprotected.

The long-range inaccuracy and slow rate of fire of the large guns led to the development of smaller-bore, rapid-firing guns. The 'quick-firers,' which eventually ranged up to 152 mm (6 in) in size, used fast-acting breech mechanisms and metal cartridges with pre-packed charges to permit very rapid loading; their shells were small enough for a single man to handle, which also contributed to a high rate of fire. In theory, a ship armed with quick-firing guns – if it could close in – could smother a battleship in fire before the latter could get off a fatal reply. For a time it seemed that lightly armoured ships, such as protected cruisers, carrying multiple batteries of quick-firing guns might challenge the supremacy of the big battleships. In the event, however, the obvious counter was adopted of adding quick-firing guns to the battleships' inventory. At the same time, much effort was devoted to increasing the rate of fire of the largest guns. It turned out, for example, that merely training gun crews to load more rapidly could increase the rate of fire of a 305 mm (12 in) gun from once every two or three minutes to two shots per minute.

During the 1880s technical improvements in the quality of armour made it possible to resist even heavy shells with plates thin enough (and therefore light enough) to spread over much of the hull, and lighter armour sufficient to keep out shells of the quick-firers could be spread over much of the side of the new ships. In the last decade of the century battleship design in all navies had settled to a standard type in which two or four heavy guns of 305 or 343 mm (12 or 13.5 in) were supplemented by a battery of quick-firing weapons of about 152 mm (6 in) size; machine guns or very light cannon were also installed to resist torpedo-boat attack.

Marksmanship

This standard type had evolved almost without the benefit of combat experience. The first major naval battles after Lissa were fought between the obsolescent fleets of China and Japan in 1894–5, and served only to underline the value of the quick-firer. Three years later the United States fought Spain, but in both the major engagements of that war– at Manila Bay (Philippines) and off Havana (Cuba) – the Spanish fleet proved quite unprepared for battle. Indeed, the major lesson of the Spanish-American War was the very low standard of marksmanship of the U.S. fleet, and especially of the crews of the battleship guns. This suggested that, unless the accuracy of the large guns and the marksmanship of their gunners improved drastically, small ships with quick-firing guns ought to stand a good chance against battleships – and that sea-going torpedo boats might do even better.

That the balance of fire-power within the fleets was not tilted that way was due, in large measure, to the efforts of a British cruiser commander, Captain Percy Scott, during the early years of the 20th century. At that time most gunners compensated for the roll of a moving ship in much the same way as Nelson's gunners had done at Trafalgar: they tried to fire their guns at the exact moment in the roll of the ship when the gun was aligned with the target. Scott found that gunners who attempted to compensate for roll by continuously working the gun's elevating gear were on target for more of the time. He also moved the aiming telescope to a position on the gun where its operator was well clear of the weapon's recoil; this permitted

The French *D'Entrecasteaux* (1899) was typical of the protected cruisers of its era, with no hull armour but with thickened steel decks and internal steel bulkheads. Of 8,114 tons and armed with two 240 mm (9.4 in) and twelve 138 mm (5.4 in) guns, she was intended for use as a commerce raider.

'continuous-aim' firing – and the results were dramatic. Under Scott's direction, his cruiser *Scylla's* six 120 mm (4.7 in) guns scored 56 hits out of 70 rounds fired at a target – a score of 80 per cent, compared to the fleet average of about 35 per cent. The ship's score firing her 152 mm (6 in) guns was equally impressive.

In spite of initial Admiralty resistence, Scott's improvements were to revolutionize gunnery in the Royal Navy. His ideas were to be taken up and developed during the early years of the 20th century by Lieutenant William S. Sims of the U.S. Navy.

The Big Ships

The efforts of Scott and Sims (both of whom would achieve flag rank in their respective navies) led to the revival and improvement of the big gun and, indirectly, of the battleship itself during this period, especially in face of the threat posed by self-propelled torpedoes.

During the 1880s a remarkable range of battleship designs had appeared in the European navies. Some had very little freeboard, like monitors, and mounted only a couple of immense turrets; others, known as barbette ships, had their guns high above water and unprotected by armour. Some ships had no side armour, one theory being that the extra speed possible without the weight of armour would present a more difficult target for enemy guns. The disposition of the main armament also varied widely on battleships; some experts argued that all the guns of the main batteries should be along the ship's centre-line, while others argued for 'wing' turrets on either side of the ship's superstructure. Secondary guns might be turret mounted or sited at casemates in the side of the hull.

This apparently random collection of ship designs shook down very rapidly, partly as a result of the example shown by the Royal Navy in its introduction of the *Royal Sovereign* class, designed in 1889, which became the standard for subsequent designs in most navies until 1905. The only major developments around the turn of the century were vast improvements in the long-range accuracy and rate of fire of the heavy guns. Battles could be fought at ranges at which lighter weapons would be far less effective, so that the array of 152 mm (6 in) quick-firers lost much of its value. Long-range engage-

ments were in any case attractive because of the growing threat of the self-propelled torpedo, fired by battleships as well as by lesser craft. All navies now began to upgrade secondary-gun batteries on battleships. The Royal Navy installed 190 mm (7.5 in) and even 234 mm (9.2 in) secondary guns to support the 305 mm (12 in) main battery. In the United States, 203 mm (8 in) intermediate guns had been mounted in a few ships in the 1890s, and then dropped in later designs, but the performance of these guns in battle against the Spanish revived the practice, and by 1905 the United States was building battleships with 305 mm (12 in) main batteries, 203 mm (8 in) intermediate, and 178 mm (7 in) secondary batteries. This combination may seem ludicrous, but there was in fact a considerable difference in weight (and destructive power) between the intermediate and secondary shells: the 203 mm shells weighed 113 kg (250 lb) and the 178 mm weighed 77 kg (170 lb).

As the battleships evolved, so did the cruisers. In the 1860s there had been three types of cruisers. The first type was used to keep the imperial peace in distant waters, their ability to shell a local port or to land marines being their main military rationale. A second type was used in trade warfare – that is, for attacking or protecting merchant ships. Such cruisers had to be fast since some merchantmen, especially passenger liners, had a fair turn of speed. Finally, cruisers were used by the battle fleets as fast scouts and as messengers (radio was still in the future).

By the 1880s these types had been resolved into two main categories – the protected cruiser and the armoured cruiser. The protected cruiser, intended primarily for peace-keeping and for commerce raiding or protection in distant waters, had no side armour but its underwater equipment was protected by thick steel decks and by steel bulkheads that divided the hull lengthwise into watertight compartments. The armoured cruiser became a practical proposition when improvement in the quality of armour allowed a considerable reduction in the thickness (and therefore weight) of the armour belts on hulls. Armoured cruisers had side belts about 152 mm (6 in) thick. Although lacking the fire-power of battleships, they were almost as large and were considerably faster and more manoeuvrable. They could

HMS *Royal Sovereign* (1891) was one of the most highly regarded battleships of the last years of the 19th century, more than 50 British and foreign ships being influenced by her design. Her high freeboard enabled her to sail at speed and to fire her largest guns in heavy seas.

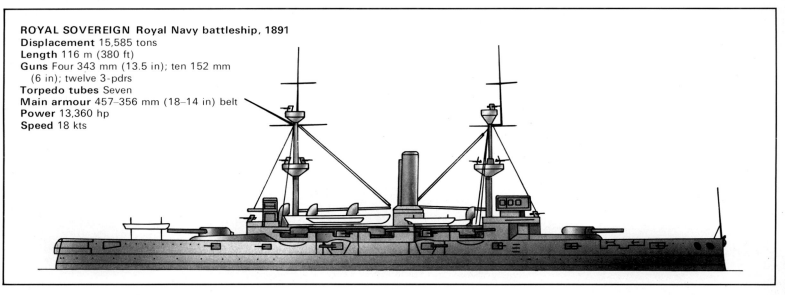

ROYAL SOVEREIGN Royal Navy battleship, 1891
Displacement 15,585 tons
Length 116 m (380 ft)
Guns Four 343 mm (13.5 in); ten 152 mm
  (6 in); twelve 3-pdrs
Torpedo tubes Seven
Main armour 457–356 mm (18–14 in) belt
Power 13,360 hp
Speed 18 kts

be used to form a fast squadron in a battle fleet or, individually, as formidable raiders.

Toward the close of the 19th century, then, major navies consisted mainly of battleships supported by large armoured cruisers as well as numerous lesser protected cruisers for subsidiary duties. It was just at this time, however, that the virtues of this simple organization were challenged by improvements in the propulsion and destructive power of the torpedo.

Torpedo Boats and Destroyers
As we have seen, during the American Civil War quite impressive warships had been sunk by small charges of explosive set off below the waterline, albeit sometimes at the cost of the lives of the sailors making the attack. It was soon argued that if the charges could be detonated by remote control, such mines would represent a weapon that was both cheap and capable of sinking or disabling the largest warships. Whitehead's self-propelled torpedo of 1868 established the basic principles for this type of weapon. But it was unreliable, tended to deviate from its course and depth, and was too slow to counter the effect of a ship taking evasive action. From the mid-1870s, however, torpedoes underwent slow but steady development, including the use of contra-rotating propellers and gyroscope to improve directional stability, and more powerful engines. By the mid-1890s torpedoes could carry a 135 kg (300 lb) warhead at speeds of up to 55 km/h (30 knots) and had a range of up to 3.5 km (2 miles).

The potential of torpedoes was enhanced by the development of a new type of vessel to deliver them, and the first torpedo boats – small craft with a good turn of speed – began to appear in the late 1870s. The early boats, although useful for coastal duties, were not seaworthy enough to pose a threat to battleships and cruisers on the high seas. But the long-term danger they posed was recognized, and countermeasures had to be devised. The answer was the 'torpedo-boat destroyer' – a type originally specified by Rear-Admiral John Fisher (then Britain's Third Sea Lord) in 1893; the name of such vessels was soon shortened to 'destroyer.' The first of these ships were essentially enlarged torpedo boats; but they were faster than their prey and, more important, they were sufficiently seaworthy to sail with the large ships of the battle fleet. They gradually increased in size and were armed not only with light guns for hunting torpedo boats but also with torpedoes. In short, they evolved two roles: as torpedo-boat killers and (with their own torpedoes) as fleet-attack vessels and scouts.

By the early years of the 20th century, then, it was assumed that a major high-seas engagement would begin with the sighting of one battle fleet by the other's scouts. By this time, radio communication had been developed and scouting over the horizon was possible. The fleets would then form up parallel to each other in line ahead at a range of several miles, each ship firing at one or more of the enemy ships directly opposite. The advantage of broadside engagement was that it enabled ships to fire all their heavy guns at once. Given evenly matched fleets, the outcome of such broadside engagements hinged upon the quality of their gunnery. The object, obviously, was to sink as many enemy vessels as possible. But it was almost equally advantageous to cripple some of them. If this happened, the entire enemy fleet would have to slow down so that the damaged ones could keep pace with the rest – and this gave the opposing fleet the chance to execute the manoeuvre known as 'crossing the T.' This involved pulling ahead of the enemy fleet, and then cutting across its path at right angles. The value of this manoeuvre was that, as each ship crossed the T in turn, it could pour a broadside into the leading enemy ships, while the latter could respond only with their forward gun turrets. If neither battle fleet managed to cross the T during the day, destroyers could be used to make torpedo attacks under cover of darkness, with the hope of disabling a number of vessels so that the manoeuvre could be carried out the following day.

By the end of the 1870s improvements in torpedo design had led to the development of the small, fast, steam-powered torpedo boat. Over 100 were built in Britain between 1879 and 1903. *No 42* (1889) had torpedo launchers fore and aft and was about 40 m (130 ft) in length.

Submarines

Although the destroyer seemed to offer an effective answer to the torpedo boat, the torpedo itself remained a potentially devastating weapon against ships of every size. The invention of the submarine was greatly to enhance its power. The first submarine to incorporate a launching tube for a Whitehead torpedo was built in 1885 by the Swedish inventor Thorsten Nordenfeldt. The main problem in developing submarines was how to power them when submerged; it was impossible to use steam or internal-combustion engines since both require air. The answer was an electric motor, and the first successful submarine with this type of engine was the French *Gustave Zédé* of 1893. An American submarine designed by John Holland followed in 1895, and the Royal Navy bought several Holland-type subs in 1901; the latter were the first to have periscopes. In Britain, the Holland-types gave way to the series of 'A', 'B', 'C', and 'D' classes – the last of which, in 1910, featured a conning tower, external ballast tanks, and 457 mm (18 in) torpedo tubes; for surface cruising the 'D' class was powered by diesel engines, which were also used to charge the batteries of the electric motor.

Birth of the Dreadnought

The first few years of the 20th century saw the final stages in the evolution of the battleship. In any major engagement at sea it was recognized that battleships, rather than cruisers or destroyers, would play the decisive role owing to the destructive power of their largest guns. At that time, three central issues dominated the controversy about the design of the 'ideal' battleship. The first issue was the relative importance of speed, armament, and protective armour, and which of these three elements should be given priority. For a given engine power, high speed and heavy armour were clearly incompatible – but it was argued that a fast ship needed less armour because she would be more difficult to hit. On the other hand, the increasing power, range, and accuracy of the big guns put a premium on defensive armour as well as speed – and in any case the immense weight of the big guns was also a factor in a battleship's speed and manoeuvrability. The second issue had to do with the nature of the armament: whether to have a mixture of big 305 mm (12 in) guns and intermediate and secondary batteries, or to concentrate entirely on the big guns. The third issue was that of the size of battleships – an issue that had to do not only with limited national budgets but also with the question of whether a few very large, and therefore faster, vessels were superior in fighting power to a larger number of smaller, slower, less heavily armoured ones.

In 1903 these issues were crystallised by the brilliant Italian engineer and designer Vittorio Cuniberti in an article in *Jane's Fighting Ships*. Cuniberti argued the case for a battleship armed only with 12 guns of 305 mm (12 in) size, protected with 305 mm (12 in) armour, and capable of very high speed. The article aroused enormous controversy in admiralties all over the world. The following year, however, the outbreak of the Russo-Japanese War provided an opportunity to assess the validity of Cuniberti's views.

The first high-seas engagement of this war occurred on 10 August 1904 in the Yellow Sea. It was a somewhat desultory affair, but significant in that the Russians opened fire at a range of no less than 17 km (10.5 miles) – a distance far beyond the effective range of contemporary intermediate or secondary guns. Morover,

The first wholly British submarines, the 'A' class (1904–5), evolved from the smaller American Holland designs. The *A6* seen here displaced about 180 tons and was 28.7 m (94 ft) long. She had two 457 mm (18 in) torpedo tubes, and could make 11.5 kts on the surface and 7 kts submerged.

these opening salvoes from the Russian 305 mm (12 in) guns scored very near misses on two of the Japanese battleships. The fleets gradually closed to about 12 km (7.5 miles), at which range the Japanese flagship was struck close to the waterline and suffered severe damage. Later, at slightly shorter range, the Russian flagship was hit twice by Japanese 305 mm shells.

In the decisive naval engagement of the war, the Battle of Tsushima Strait (which separates Korea and mainland Japan) in May 1905, the Japanese annihilated the Russian fleet. Although many of the Russian ships were finally despatched at about 3 km (1.9 miles) or less most of them had been crippled previously by salvoes from the Japanese 305 mm shells at far greater range.

One of the important lessons of both the 1904 and 1905 engagements was that not only were the big guns the decisive element but that, at long range, the intermediate and secondary guns were actually a hindrance, because the splashes made by their shells tended to confuse the aim of the gunlayers of the main batteries. The problem had already been stressed by Percy Scott, who for long had argued the vital importance of accurate shell spotting if effective corrections to aim were to be made.

Of all the men to be influenced by Cuniberti's theories, the most significant was Admiral Sir John Fisher, who became Britain's First Sea Lord in 1904. The following year he ordered the construction of a capital ship that was to establish the basic configuration of all subsequent battleships. That ship was HMS *Dreadnought*, which was rushed from keel-laying to completion in the astonishing time of one year. She was launched at Portsmouth dockyard in February 1906.

With a displacement of 21,845 tons and a length of 160 m (526 ft), the *Dreadnought* was considerably larger than any previous British warship. She was the first modern battleship to have an all-big-gun armament – 10 guns of 305 mm (12 inch) in twin turrets. Three of the turrets were on the centreline – one forward and two aft – and the other two were on each side of the superstructure amidships, allowing an eight-gun broadside on either beam. Her only other armament was 27 76 mm (12 pdr) light guns and five 457 mm (18 in) torpedo tubes. Her main side armour was 203-280 mm (8-11 in)

Left Anti-torpedo nets on a British battlecruiser, about 1912. In World War I the nets were easily pierced by torpedoes and were soon abandoned.

Below Typical of the last-generation pre-dreadnoughts was HMS *King Edward VII* (1903) of 16,350 tons. She had a mixed armament of main, intermediate, and secondary guns.

Bottom HMS *Dreadnought*, combining an all-big-gun armament with high-speed steam-turbine engines, made every existing battleship obsolete at her launching.

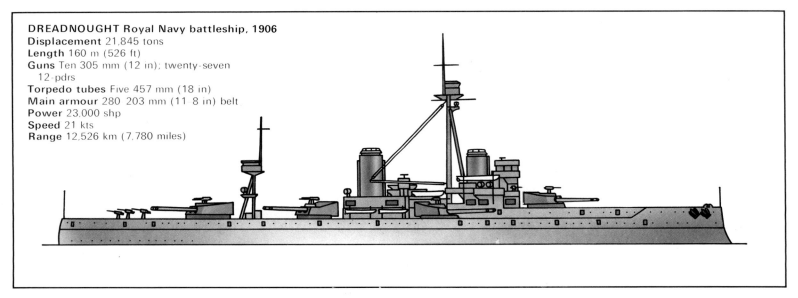

DREADNOUGHT Royal Navy battleship, 1906
Displacement 21,845 tons
Length 160 m (526 ft)
Guns Ten 305 mm (12 in); twenty-seven 12-pdrs
Torpedo tubes Five 457 mm (18 in)
Main armour 280 203 mm (11 8 in) belt
Power 23,000 shp
Speed 21 kts
Range 12,526 km (7,780 miles)

Top HMS *Invincible* (1907), the first true battlecruiser. The type was as heavily armed as a dreadnought, but its lighter armour gave it an advantage in speed.

Centre The USS *Michigan* (16,000 tons) and her sister ship, the *South Carolina*, were laid down before the *Dreadnought* but completed only in 1910. Unlike the British battleship they had superimposed turrets fore and aft, all on the centre-line.

Bottom The *Dante Alighieri* (1913), one of the first Italian dreadnoughts, displaced 21,800 tons and could make over 24 kts. She was the first battleship to have triple-gun main turrets.

thick, and the interior of her hull was divided into watertight compartments with steel bulkheads. The most daring innovation was the use of steam turbine engines instead of the conventional reciprocating (piston) engines. Marine turbines had been developed by Charles Parsons and first demonstrated in public in 1897. By 1905 the Royal Navy had installed them only in two destroyers, and to specify their use in an immense new battleship was an act of remarkable daring and faith. In the event they were triumphantly successful. Developing no less than 23,000 shp, they allowed the *Dreadnought* to cruise continuously at the very high speed of 21 knots – about 39 km/h (24 mph). Although earlier battleships had been nominally capable of up to 19 kts, their reciprocating engines vibrated so badly at such speeds that their normal cruising speed was nearer 12 kts.

The *Dreadnought* was a sensation: at a stroke

she had rendered obsolete all capital ships in every navy. From Britain's point of view the advantage was more apparent than real: ironically, since she had the largest and most powerful capital-ship fleet in the world, Britain stood to lose her ascendancy unless her unrivalled shipbuilding experience enabled her to keep ahead in the world race to adopt *Dreadnought*-type battleships.

Two of the first dreadnoughts (as the type came to be called) to appear outside Britain were the USS *South Carolina* and *Michigan* of 17,900 tons, armed with eight 305 mm (12 in) guns in four twin turrets (two fore and two aft) on the centreline. They were, indeed, designed before HMS *Dreadnought*, and owed much to the thinking of men such as William Sims, who had also taken Cuniberti's precepts to heart; but they were laid down after the *Dreadnought* and were launched only in 1910.

Fisher's fascination with speed and firepower tended to be at the expense of the third element, armour. The *Dreadnought* and her British successors were more lightly, or at least less effectively, armoured than some of their counterparts in other navies. Indeed, Fisher believed that there was a significant role for large, ultra-fast vessels with armament comparable to dreadnoughts but protected with minimal armour. Such ships would reconnoitre ahead of the battle fleet and would be capable of destroying the reconnaissance cruisers of the enemy. The concept found its first expression in the *Invincible* class. The first of such ships was HMS *Invincible* (1907) of 17,370 tons. She was capable of 26 kts, was armed with eight 305 mm (12 in) guns, and had a 152 mm (6 in) armour belt. Originally called a heavy armoured cruiser, the type was to become known by the more familiar name of battlecruiser.

By the middle of the Edwardian era Britain's main rival in what was developing into a massive European naval build-up was Germany. The Germans were faced with much the same facts of technology as was Fisher, but they drew somewhat different conclusions from them. They placed a premium on the survivability of their ships in battle. If they fought the British, they would be outnumbered; but if their ships could survive the battle, they could return for repairs. They chose, therefore, to sacrifice maximum gun calibre in favour of greater armour protection, not only in their battleships but also in their battlecruisers. Typical of the latter was the *Von der Tann* (1909), of 19,100 tons, which had eight 280 mm (11 in) guns, a 254 mm (10 in) armour belt, and could cruise at 24 kts. Ironically, this choice left both fleets fairly evenly matched: the smaller guns of the Germans could do about as well against the weaker armour of the British as the more powerful guns of the latter could do against the Germans' heavier armour. In certain areas of technology the Germans undoubtedly had the edge. Their armour-piercing shells were inherently superior, and they spent a great deal of effort in perfecting a type that would penetrate thick armour before exploding. Although John Jellicoe, who would command the British Grand Fleet in 1914, complained of the defects in British armour-piercing shells as early as 1910, little was done to remedy the situation, and the

Royal Navy suffered badly as a consequence in World War I.

The battleship continued to develop in the years after 1906 as every navy poured most of its shipbuilding budget into new capital-ship construction. The size of the big guns gradually increased to 381 mm (15 in) in the British and German navies and, in 1916, to 406 mm (16 in) in the United States' and Japanese. Machinery improvements promised the possibility of a fast battleship, and here, as in the original *Dreadnought*, British boldness was shown. In 1911 projections of the German building programme suggested that by 1914 the Germans would have a fast-battleship division with a speed as great as 23 kts. The British Naval War College pointed out that a 25 kt battleship division would be able to cross the 'T' of the German fleet. Heavily enough armed, such a fast division might well be decisive in battle. In 1912 Winston Churchill, First Lord of the Admiralty, decided to build just such a division. This resulted in the *Queen Elizabeth* class, typified by the celebrated HMS *Warspite* (1915) of 33,020 tons, which in various forms was to see distinguished service in both world wars.

High speed required the use of oil fuel rather than the usual coal. Coal was not as efficient as oil and, moreover, it created an ash that had to be cleared from the boilers every few hours in high-speed steaming. In addition, coaling was a slow, back-breaking task. On the other hand, although good reserves of steam coal existed in the British Isles, oil would have to be brought from overseas, which might prove difficult in wartime. Churchill felt that this risk was worthwhile; to ensure the supply of oil he invested heavily in Middle Eastern oilfields, laying the foundation for British influence in that region over the next five decades.

He took one other remarkable step. In 1911 British battleships were being armed with a new 343 mm (13.5 in) gun, usually mounted in five twin turrets. One of these turrets would have to be foregone if the 60,000 or 70,000 shp engines required for 25 kts were to fit within a battleship hull. Churchill resolved to redress this loss in firepower by going to the next calibre, 381 mm (15 in); at one move, the weight of a shell rose from 635 to 871 kg (1,400 to 1,920 lb). The risk lay in the fact that the 381 mm gun was as yet no more than a paper design. Guns had been known to fail, even after promising tests (the very-high-velocity 305 mm guns of some British dreadnoughts had proved appallingly inaccurate). However, to await completion of a full test programme would have meant delaying construction of the new ships. The aim was to have them completed by 1914 – a critical date that would mark the opening of the reconstructed Kiel Canal, which would allow German dreadnoughts to pass freely between the Baltic and North seas without having to sail around Denmark. Churchill decided to press ahead. One gun was rushed to completion, and its tests proved most gratifying. The gamble had paid off.

The *Dreadnought's* successors and their oil-burning turbine engines completely remade the fleets of the world between 1906 and 1914. While there was no equivalent revolution in light cruisers or destroyers (although the latter steadily increased in size), the speed of the new battleships and battlecruisers required a similar increase in the speed of their auxiliaries. No light cruiser or destroyer built much before 1910 was still a first-line ship four years later. Once more, a naval revolution had proceeded on the basis of untested theories; but the trial was soon to come.

Eugene B. Ely became the first pilot to take off from a ship when he flew this Curtiss pusher biplane off the specially converted deck of USS *Birmingham* in Hampton Roads, Virginia, in November 1910. The following January he landed, took off, and landed again on the cruiser *Pennsylvania*.

CHAPTER 4
WORLD WAR 1

World War I is an excellent illustration of the adage that new technology breeds totally unexpected consequences. On land, few experts predicted that the invention of the machine-gun and barbed wire would lead to a drawn-out, bloody stalemate in the trenches. At sea, the submarine failed to fulfil the expectation of its original inventors that it would destroy battle fleets – but it succeeded in a totally different direction. The great battle fleets that had consumed the bulk of the British and German naval budgets saw relatively little action, and the few major fleet battles proved surprisingly inconclusive. And the radio and the aeroplane played major, if largely unsung, roles.

Perhaps the greatest surprise was the overall character of the war at sea. War against merchant shipping, as it was understood before 1914, involved attempts to stop the flow of contraband (war supplies) into an enemy country. Ships not carrying contraband could not legitimately be stopped. A ship suspected of carrying contraband, however, could be intercepted and any war cargo confiscated; the ship would then be sent into a friendly or neutral port under a prize crew and sold.

Clearly, then, anti-trade warfare was the work of fast surface ships, which could run down their quarry and force it to heave-to while boarding parties made their searches. In 1914 Britain planned to starve Germany and her allies of essential war material by declaring a blockade of German ports and searching ships on passage to them. The existence of mines and submarines made a close blockade impractical; but German shipping had to pass either to the north of Scotland or through the English Channel, where it could be stopped for examination. As the war progressed Britain gradually extended the list of contraband on the theory that the only thing that would knock Germany out of the conflict would be the total destruction of her economy. Although it was not conclusive, the British blockade contributed materially to the eventual German defeat.

The German approach to trade warfare was far more practical. At first, German cruisers that had been based in overseas colonies carried on anti-trade war, forcing the British to detach large forces of their own to hunt them down. The most spectacularly successful of these ships was the light cruiser *Emden* (4,150 tons), which sank or captured 23 merchantmen in less than two months in the Indian Ocean before the Australian cruiser *Sydney* finally sank her off the Cocos Islands in November 1914. (A key element in the *Sydney*'s success, and an important foreshadowing of later operations, was the use of direction-finders to locate the *Emden* when she used her radio.)

Coronel and the Falklands

Far more threatening, even if less successful, was the German Pacific Squadron, under Admiral Maximilian Graf von Spee, consisting of two large armoured cruisers, the *Scharnhorst* and *Gneisenau*, both of 12,780 tons, as well as the light cruisers *Nürnberg*, *Leipzig*, and *Dresden*. At the outbreak of war Spee's force had been on a training cruise in the Caroline Islands. It then sailed eastward across the Pacific, planning to prey on British trade routes along the western coast of South America. Off Coronel, about 450 km (280 miles) south of the Chilean city of Valparaiso, it was met by a British squadron commanded by Rear-Admiral Sir Christopher Cradock in November 1914. Cradock's force consisted of the armoured cruisers *Good Hope* (14,000 tons) and *Monmouth* (9,800 tons), the light cruiser *Glasgow*, and an armed merchantman, the *Otranto*. Both of the British armoured cruisers were manned largely by reservists, and the greatly superior gunnery of the Germans soon sent the *Good Hope* and *Monmouth* to the bottom. This was a serious setback, since South American goods, such as Argentine beef, were very important to Britain. Indeed, it was important enough for two battle-cruisers – the *Invincible* and *Inflexible*, each of 17,370 tons and armed with eight 305 mm (12 in) guns – to be detached from the main British fleet and sent to join a force of four armoured cruisers and two light cruisers off the east coast of South America. This was, indeed, the only time in the war when battlecruisers operated in their originally conceived role of armoured-cruiser killers, and they performed it quite well, if at an inordinate cost in ammunition expended, off the Falkland Islands on 8 December 1914. The two German armoured cruisers and two of the light cruisers were sunk. The *Dresden* escaped, only to be caught and sunk five months later by the *Glasgow*.

The Submarine War

With the failure of these and other surface raiders, the Germans were reduced to using their submarine force against merchant ships. Before the war few experts had given much thought to the precise role of submarines. It was assumed they might be used as torpedo boats in coastal defence, and also as coastal pickets to give warning of enemy fleet movements. But they had not seriously been envisaged as a weapon against merchantmen. As we have seen, ships suspected of carrying contraband could be stopped and searched. Submarines are far from ideal for such work: to send men aboard a merchantman, a sub would have to remain on the surface for a considerable time, and it would be highly vulnerable to attack – especially if the merchantman happened to be equipped with a gun. Thus, although international law expressly forbade an attack on a merchant ship without adequate warning, anti-trade submarines would be almost useless if employed in any other manner.

At first the Germans used their submarines against warships, and only occasionally against merchant ships in the prescribed manner. The start of the German submarine campaign was dramatic. On 22 September 1914, in little more than a half-hour, the 450-ton submarine *U-9* sank three British light cruisers off the Belgian coast. More than 1,200 British officers and ratings died in the triple sinking.

The early German U (*untersee* = under-sea) boat successes were achieved both with torpedoes and with secretly laid mines. But it was soon determined that surface warships steaming at even moderate cruising speeds made elusive targets, especially if they were zig-zagging, which made it more difficult for the U-boat commander to reach a firing position. Slow merchant ships were easier targets, and in 1915, in an effort to break out of the frustrating

The British battlecruisers *Invincible* and (on the right) *Inflexible* overwhelm the German armoured cruisers *Scharnhorst* and *Gneisenau* at the Battle of the Falkland Islands in December 1914. The two battlecruisers had been detached from the Home Fleet, and they amply avenged the defeat of Rear-Admiral Cradock's squadron off Coronel a month before.

Right A torpedo from the *U-35* strikes an Allied merchantman in the Mediterranean in April 1917. At this time submarines invariably surfaced before launching torpedoes against unarmed merchant ships.

Above U-boat crewmen check a torpedo before launching it. Torpedoes commonly had two contra-rotating propellers.

Above right American mass-production techniques were applied to several classes of warships from late 1917 onwards. The destroyer *Ward*, shown on the stocks at the Mare Island Navy Yard (N.Y.), was launched two weeks after keel-laying.

stalemate in the land war, the Germans declared a submarine blockade of the British Isles. They would somehow determine (in other words, arbitrarily decide) which ships were carrying contraband, and such ships would be sunk on sight. This was 'unrestricted submarine warfare'; it was strongly condemned by neutrals such as the United States, particularly after the *U-20* sank the huge unarmed Cunard liner *Lusitania* on 7 May 1915, with 128 Americans among the 1,198 lives that were lost.

Following the protest after the *Lusitania* outrage, the Germans largely ceased attacking merchant ships without warning and reverted to the policy of stopping and searching them. The British adopted ingenious measures to frustrate them. One successful idea was the 'Q' ships – innocent-looking merchant vessels, crewed by Royal Navy men in mufti and armed with concealed guns.

Faced with these and other countermeasures to their anti-trade submarines, the Germans turned once more to unrestricted submarine warfare, which some of their naval strategists claimed might starve Britain out of the war within a few months. However, the threat of the United States entering the war on the British side caused yet another reversion to 'conventional' submarine use in 1916.

By the beginning of 1917, both sides were becoming desperate. As early as 1915 the disastrous failure of the Dardanelles campaign against the Turkish forces (see page 42) suggested that the Allies would be unable to

outflank the Central Powers by attacking them from the east. On the other hand, Austrian failures in the south suggested to the Germans that they would soon bear almost the entire weight of war on two fronts. The Germans began to think in terms of ultimate expedients. They suspected that quite soon the Americans would enter the war no matter what they did. Thus, in January 1917 the German government once again ordered unrestricted submarine warfare. (This did not actually bring in the Americans, but another desperate German initiative did: the Zimmermann, telegram, in which the Germans promised to aid Mexico in reconquering the provinces she had lost to the United States in 1848 in return for Mexican help in the war. The telegram was intercepted and decoded by British cipher experts.)

The new German submarine offensive came close to success. By 1917 Germany possessed a large and well-seasoned corps of submariners who were sinking one in every four merchant ships destined for British ports. Three years of Allied efforts had produced no device that could easily detect submarines underwater, and therefore the chief Allied tactic of patrolling areas in which submarine attack could be expected was generally fruitless. The alternative was to lure the submarines into sea areas in which anti-submarine ships were concentrated. This was the concept of convoying, in which merchant ships sailed in large groups, with warships in close attendance. The convoy strategy was strongly opposed on the theory that merely assembling fleets of merchantmen in British and foreign ports would add so much to port delays as effectively to decrease sharply an already badly depleted Allied merchant marine. Moreover, it seemed almost defeatist merely to escort merchant ships instead of using warships aggressively to hunt submarines.

Convoying was suggested several times in 1917 but was rejected until it was very forcefully advocated by the U.S. Navy in the person of William Sims, who was now the admiral commanding U.S. naval forces which began to arrive in British waters soon after the United States entered the war in April 1917. Sims was able to provide U.S. destroyers to assist in escort operations, and later the United States built large numbers of wooden sub-chasers for inshore patrols, as well as many destroyers. The convoy proved effective because it overcame the problem of the invisibility of the submarine. Once a submarine attacked, a destroyer could race back along the track of its torpedoes, dropping depth charges over the apparent position of the submarine. Moreover, concentrating the ships into convoys cleared vast areas of the seas of shipping, so that even on an extended cruise a U-boat might fail to sight a target.

Naval aeroplanes and airships were beginning to make a major, if indirect, contribution to the war against submarines by 1917. In principle, aircraft were most useful for their ability to spot submarines on the surface. Submarines had a very limited underwater endurance, and moreover could move much faster on the surface. Because they were small and lay low in the water, they could be certain of sighting surface ships well before they themselves became visible, and they could always dive to avoid attack. However, their small size did not protect them from detection from the air, and by 1917 large flying boats could even carry bombs with which to attack them. Thus, whenever an aircraft appeared a submarine would have to dive. Air patrols in fact sank very few U-boats; but by forcing them to 'keep their heads down' they helped to neutralize them as a danger to merchant ships. Convoying had a similar effect, since the U-boats could often surface only for brief moments before being pursued by the escorting warships.

During World War I a far greater tonnage of shipping was destroyed by torpedoes (mainly submarine-launched) and mines than by gunfire. The use of convoys helped to counter the threat of U-boats to Allied merchant ships from mid-1917 onwards. These merchantman in the English Channel were dazzle-painted to make them a more difficult target for enemy submarines.

WORLD WAR I SUBMARINE CAMPAIGN

Merchant Losses to German U-Boats

	1914–1915	1916	1917	1918 (10 months)
British Merchant Ships	231	288	1052	527
British Fishing Vessels	168	134	200	76
Allied Merchant Ships	76	344	708	314
Neutral Merchant Ships	93	332	679	186
Totals	568	1098	2639	1103

German U-Boats Lost*

	1914–1915	1916	1917	1918 (10 months)
	24	25	66	88

* At the end of the war 138 U-boats were surrendered to the Allies.

The German High Seas Fleet in 1914. Leading is the *Nassau* (20,210 tons), completed in 1909. The four battleships in this class had a main armament of twelve 280 mm (11 in) guns mounted in two turrets on the centre-line fore and aft and in four wing turrets.

The Big-Ship Battles

This was hardly the sort of sea war that might have been predicted, given the large battleship-building programmes of the major powers. Indeed, the war had begun with fleet operations on a large scale, and even with a demonstration of the significance of a single large ship. In 1914 the Germans had the modern battlecruiser *Goeben* (22,640 tons) in the Mediterranean. Cut off from her home base, she nevertheless threatened the stream of transports the French were using to move their North African colonial troops to the European front. She also threatened the vital trade links of the Mediterranean, and even before the outbreak of hostilities British naval units in the Mediterranean were ordered to shadow her with a view to sinking her if war was declared. At the outbreak of hostilities the *Goeben* steamed eastward at high speed, evading first a pair of British battlecruisers, and then a cruiser squadron. For a time it seemed that the German ship would make for the Austrian bases on the Adriatic, but instead she steamed into the Dardanelles, where she was formally handed over to Turkey, which shortly entered the war on the German side. Crewed by Germans (who wore the fez because they were officially in Turkish service), and in a plan known only to the Sultan and his closest advisers, the *Goeben* steamed into the Black Sea and shelled the Russian seaport of Odessa. Russia declared war, and the Dardanelles (at the north-eastern end of the Aegean Sea) was closed to her extensive wheat trade – and to Allied efforts to supply the vast Russian armies.

In 1915 the British tried to force a passage of the Dardanelles. After several of their older battleships had been sunk by mines, the British landed troops at Gallipoli, at the northern end of the strait. The campaign, the largest amphibious operation of the war, ended in bloody disaster. Its political consequences included the dismissal of Churchill as First Lord of the Admiralty.

In the North Sea, the Germans realized that the main arm of their navy, the High Seas Fleet, could not defeat the larger British Grand Fleet. Before the war they had believed that the mere existence of their fleet would tend to deter the British, on the theory that the loss of the British Navy could lead to the loss of the British Empire. Indeed, it was said of Admiral Sir John Jellicoe, commander of the Grand Fleet, that he was the only man who could lose the war in an afternoon. However, to exact this victory would almost certainly require the sacrifice of the German High Seas Fleet, and this the Kaiser was unwilling to do.

To begin with, then, the Germans sent out squadrons of battlecruisers with the aim of cutting off small British formations, and they began a policy of shelling British coastal towns, such as Hartlepool, in hopes of luring out just such groups, with the main German fleet waiting nearby to pounce. The British for their part began to station a strong force of battlecruisers nearer the German bases, in the hope that they would be able to force an action. On 24 January 1915 the two forces collided in the Battle of the Dogger Bank. The German battlecruiser squadron, commanded by Vice-Admiral Franz von Hipper in the 28,550-ton *Seydlitz*, included the largest of the German armoured cruisers, the *Blücher*, fast but under-armed and under-armoured. As the British battlecruisers, led by Admiral David Beatty in HMS *Lion* (29,680 tons), came within range, their crews became confused, and they were unable to distribute their fire effectively among the German ships. However, two German ships were damaged almost at once: the *Seydlitz*, hit in a magazine and very nearly sunk, and the unfortunate *Blücher*, which capsized and went to the bottom. The *Seydlitz's* armour – thicker and better than that on most British battlecruisers – saved her from immediate disaster. She would undoubtedly have been sunk had not ludicrously incompetent signalling work on Beatty's ship not deflected her pursuers from the correct course. As it was, the *Seydlitz* and the other German vessels made good their escape.

For their part the Germans had been horrified by how close a large battlecruiser had come to destruction as a consequence of a single hit. The shell from the *Lion* had hit one of the *Seydlitz's* two aft turrets, the flash passing down the shaft to the magazine below and killing the crews of both turrets. The German Navy set to work on improving fire protection in their ships, especially in the shafts between the gun turrets and the ammunition stores, and their efforts would bear fruit at Jutland a year later.

On 31 May 1916 the German High Seas Fleet steamed into the North Sea on yet another raid; this time it was to precipitate a full fleet engagement of the type foreseen by naval strategists before the outbreak of war. Admiral Jellicoe, warned by British radio intelligence, knew that the Germans intended to come out even before they had left Kiel.

Thanks to his skill as an organizer and to the effectiveness of Admiralty intelligence, Jellicoe had led the Grand Fleet with 24 battleships and 74 lesser warships to sea before the High Seas Fleet had departed port. Separate from this main British force were six battlecruisers and their screening ships under Beatty. They were, indeed, separated not only by their bases but also by their methods and by the personalities of their commanders. Sent out to scout ahead of the Grand Fleet, Beatty's faster battlecruisers were supported by four recently completed *Queen Elizabeth*-class dreadnoughts, the fastest British battleships then in service.

The action between the British and German fleets began when scout cruisers of the battle-cruiser force steamed ahead to investigate what turned out to be a merchant ship. They met German scouts that had also steamed ahead of their force to investigate the same ship. Both groups of scouts fell back upon their respective battlecruiser forces, which were soon joined in combat. The German commander, Hipper, with only five battlecruisers, joined the fight against what he thought were six British ships of similar type. He did not realise that immediately behind Beatty's battlecruisers were the four fast battleships of Rear-Admiral Hugh Evan-Thomas. And neither Hipper nor Vice-Admiral Reinhard Scheer, commanding the High Seas Fleet, knew that over the horizon was the entire British battle fleet under Jellicoe.

As the battle began the relatively poor gunnery of the British battlecruisers told disastrously, as did the laxness of their anti-flash precautions. In the British ships too much ammunition was stowed within the turrets, in order to promote rapid fire. Moreover, the doors sealing off the turrets from the magazines below were not completely closed, again to permit rapid fire. Similar practices had been abandoned in the German Navy as a result of the near loss of the *Seydlitz*. The British battlecruisers were relatively lightly protected along the sides and on the turrets – a matter partly of economy but also a reflection of Admiral Fisher's original concept of the battlecruiser as a unique combination of high speed and great fire-power.

The shortcomings of the British battlecruisers as battle-fleet ships, rather than as commerce raiders, were starkly demonstrated at Jutland. In particular, the combination of inadequate turret armour and inadequate gunnery procedures made the ammunition magazines below the turrets appallingly vulnerable. Soon after battle was joined three 280 mm (11 in) shells from the *Von der Tann* hit the battlecruiser *Indefatigable*, which sank after a colossal explosion. Admiral Beatty was forced to withdraw while the four fast battleships came up to support him. With this reinforcement he engaged again, but soon lost the large battlecruiser *Queen Mary* to magazine explosions. His own flagship, HMS *Lion*, was saved from similar explosions by Major F.J. W. Harvey, a marine officer, who flooded her midship turret magazine at the cost of his life.

Beatty's task within the British Grand Fleet was a combination of armed scouting and the 'development' of the German battle fleet; that is, he was to draw the Germans towards the British Grand Fleet, whose guns were to decide the issue and whose whereabouts were unknown to the Germans. In this at least Beatty was successful: he lured both Hipper's battlecruiser squadron and the High Seas Fleet under Scheer into the path of Jellicoe's dreadnoughts. For a moment it must have seemed that the High Seas Fleet was doomed, since (including the force under Evan-Thomas) the British battleships outnumbered the German by 28 to 16. It was now early evening and there were still enough hours of daylight for the British gunners to inflict terrible damage on the Germans.

It must be remembered, however, that Jellicoe could not afford to take large risks. He knew that, if blockaded, the German High Seas Fleet could have little effect on the war; on the other hand, the destruction of the Grand Fleet might well lose Britain the war. Jellicoe was highly aware of the potential of the torpedo, and he had apparently been deeply impressed by a report of floating mines being dropped in the wake of

The German armoured cruiser *Blücher* (15,260 tons) capsizing after being hit by salvoes from the British battlecruiser squadron at the Battle of the Dogger Bank in January 1915.

Souvenir

OF THE

VICTORY OF JUTLAND

FOR YOUR SPLENDID WORK I THANK YOU

MAY 31ST 1916.

Jutland was scarcely the 'victory' trumpeted in this British poster. The Grand Fleet's numerical superiority (37 capital ships to the High Seas Fleet's 27) was negated by the Germans' vastly better marksmanship. However, although the Royal Navy's losses were far greater, the battle left both fleets substantially intact, so that the Royal Navy retained its advantage in fighting power.

Opposite, below Lt. S.D. Culley takes off in a Sopwith Camel from a light barge towed behind the destroyer HMS *Redoubt* in July 1918. The barge's speed of 30 kts allowed Culley to become airborne after a deck run of only a few metres. This idea was considered as a possible alternative to the aircraft carriers (mostly converted merchantmen or cruisers) that became available in the last two years of the war.

fleeing ships during the Russo-Japanese War. A gunnery expert, he tended to over-rate the armour protection of the German ships: he had, studied the design plans of the *Seydlitz* before the war – and this battlecruiser, having survived the Dogger Bank engagement, was now at sea again in Hipper's squadron.

Finally, Jellicoe knew that his vast dreadnoughts were difficult to turn and very difficult to stop rapidly. Only a month earlier, two of his battlecruisers had collided in fog, and they were still in the repair yards. Communication between ships was by flag, blinker light, and radio. The first two might prove invisible in the smoke of battle; radio was still unreliable at best. In the interest of retaining control over his unwieldy battle line, Jellicoe formulated rigid Fighting Instructions, which reduced sharply the initiative available to his captains.

At all events Admiral Scheer, the German fleet commander, suddenly found Jellicoe almost across his bows, with the British battleships making hits on his leading ships. Scheer's battlecruisers had led the line, and they now sank a third British battlecruiser, HMS *Invincible*. However, it was soon clear to Scheer that he was steaming into disaster.

Scheer turned his battleships together and

fled through the smoke. Jellicoe lost contact, but soon regained it, and Scheer became desperate. He sent his destroyers to attack with torpedoes; then his already battered battlecruisers were sent directly at the British battle line to enable his main force to escape. It seemed that the German battlecruisers were doomed. Jellicoe hesitated, however, believing that the High Seas Fleet's retreat was intended to draw the Grand Fleet over specially sown mines – or even into the path of waiting U-boats.

This was not an unforeseen possibility; Jellicoe had prepared for it, to the extent of deciding, in formulating the Fighting Instructions, to turn away from torpedo attacks. Had he followed the more conventional policy of turning *towards* the torpedoes (that is, parallel to their tracks), Jellicoe would have closed with the retreating Germans.

Here the lack of initiative of British captains told. Although some of the battleship commanders could see illuminating star shells going off a few miles astern, and some could even see German battleships, no one informed Jellicoe, and the opportunity for retaining contact through the night (looking towards a second action at dawn) was missed. Jellicoe, thinking the High Seas Fleet had escaped, placed his dreadnoughts astride what he assumed was the most likely path of German retreat; but he was wrong. Ironically, British code-breakers had intercepted Scheer's radio message indicating his course for home, but Jellicoe ignored their information because of intelligence failures earlier in the battle. During the night Scheer's fleet was involved in a series of clashes with British destroyers at the rear of the Grand Fleet, but by dawn virtually his entire force had gained the sanctuary of the Kiel minefields.

Considered as a setpiece on its own, Jutland casts a fairly bleak light on Britain's naval prowess. The Grand Fleet lost three battlecruisers, one large armour cruiser, and five destroyers, while the High Seas Fleet lost one battlecruiser (Hipper's flagship *Lützow*), one obsolete pre-dreadnought, three light cruisers, and two torpedo boats. Jellicoe's caution and, even more, inept communications within the Grand Fleet helped to put the gloss on Scheer's brilliantly executed retreat.

In a strategic sense, however, Jellicoe did win. The Grand Fleet was still largely intact, and its numerical superiority over the High Seas Fleet remained. One American journalist observed that the Germans were claiming a great victory but that, although 'the prisoner has assaulted his jailer . . . he remains in prison'. The truth of this remark was seen the following August, when the High Seas Fleet steamed once more into the North Sea. This time Zeppelin airships were used for reconnaissance, and when they spotted the Grand Fleet Scheer immediately took evasive action. Jutland proved to be the last major naval battle of the war.

Jellicoe's performance at Jutland came in for much criticism, especially among the general public thirsting for another Trafalgar. He was 'booted upstairs', becoming First Sea Lord, while Beatty – whose performances at both Dogger Bank and Jutland had been dashing, if little else – succeeded Jellicoe as commander of the Grand Fleet.

Aircraft

World War I saw an explosion in aviation technology, and most of the contending navies exploited aircraft and airships. In 1915 the Royal Navy succeeded in sinking several Turkish ships with torpedoes dropped from floatplanes, and this success suggested to Beatty that aerial torpedo attacks might incapacitate the German fleet, even if he could not lure the latter from its protected harbours. By the end of the war the British had not only several primitive aircraft carriers but also a carrier-based torpedo bomber, the Sopwith Cuckoo.

Aside from such operations, the main value of aircraft at sea was observation. As we have seen, Zeppelins attached to the German fleet spotted Jellicoe's ships and warned Scheer. Jellicoe wanted to be able to shoot them down. His primitive anti-aircraft guns lacked sufficient range, so he asked for fighters. Light aircraft could take off from short platforms built atop the turrets of battleships and battlecruisers that were sailing into a stiffish headwind. By 1918 the Grand Fleet had scores of such aircraft assigned to it, as well as observation and scouting seaplanes serviced by seaplane carriers. Indeed, aerial scouts were now considered to be far more effective than cruisers, and in 1917–8 a number of cruisers and battlecruisers were converted into carriers.

Thus, at the end of World War I the major weapons of the next war already existed in primitive form: the carrier with its fighter and offensive aircraft, the submarine, and of course the battleship with its surface consorts. Efforts to counter the submarine would soon produce asdic (sonar), which even now remains the main sensor for locating submarines. Indeed, of all the major technologies of World War II, only radar had not yet been invented.

American and German propaganda posters. The German poster compares the total tonnage of Allied merchant shipping built with the much larger tonnage sunk by U-boats in the first six months of 1918

CHAPTER 5
BETWEEN THE WARS

The battleship *Nelson* and her sister, the *Rodney*, both launched in 1925, were the only British ships ever to have 406 mm (16 in) guns and the first to have triple-gun main turrets. The main turrets were all mounted forward in order to reduce the length of the main protective belt of armour; a similar arrangement was used later in French capital ships.

At the end of World War I Britain and France were economically prostrate and were unable to continue large-scale naval shipbuilding. In Britain the major shipyards were in any case fully occupied in replacing merchant ships destroyed by German submarines during the war. In contrast, the United States emerged from the war prosperous and with an immense naval building programme. Japan, which had participated on the side of the Allies, had its own large ambitions in the Far East and a fleet-building programme to match. Her troops were entrenched in Siberia in the aftermath of the Russian Revolution, and she had extended her influence in China during the war.

It appeared to many that the American and Japanese shipbuilding programmes were aimed at each other, particularly after the bulk of the U.S. battle fleet was transferred from the Atlantic to the Pacific in 1919. At the same time the British became uncomfortably aware that their own battle fleet, almost entirely of pre-war construction, was obsolescent. They sold off many of their earlier dreadnoughts, including HMS *Dreadnought* herself, and planned a new programme, although its execution would be difficult in view of British financial problems.

The Inter-war Naval Treaties
Many believed that the Anglo-German naval arms race had been an important cause of the war. In the absence of any immediate threat, the expensive U.S. naval programme became unpopular at home. Thus, in 1921 the United States called a naval-arms-limitation conference to prevent another naval building race and, incidentally, to stabilise great-power relations in the Pacific, where many believed the next naval war would be fought. The result was the Washington Treaty of 1922. The treaty affected the symptoms but not the underlying causes of the naval arms competition; in effect, it shifted that competition into categories of ships and weapons not limited by the treaty. Its most significant consequence was to accelerate development of the aircraft carrier.

In 1922 the battleship was still considered the ultimate expression of sea power. It was also by far the most expensive, and the easiest to limit. At Washington the United States proposed the wholesale scrapping of numerous existing ships to reduce the United States, British, and Japanese fleets to a ratio of 5:5:3 in battleship tonnage, and no new ships were to be built for 10 years. This rule was later modified to permit the

United States and Japan each to finish one nearly complete battleship, and Britain to build two new ones, the sister ships *Nelson* and *Rodney* of 38,000 tons. After 10 years new battleships were to be limited in size so as to make it difficult for any power to build new ships of such power as to overwhelm existing older ones.

In order to make it impossible to get around the prohibition on new battleship construction, the Treaty also limited the size of cruisers. The limit was a very high one – 10,000 tons standard displacement and 203 mm (8 in) main armament – largely in view of the existence of several large British cruisers and also of American studies asserting the value of large cruisers for operations in the vast Pacific. One important consequence of the limit on battleship size was that, at least in 1922, it seemed that it would be impossible for anyone to build successful and well-armoured battlecruisers. (The battlecruiser HMS *Hood*, of 44,600 tons, which was completed in 1920 and was in effect a very fast battleship, greatly exceeded the treaty tonnage limit but was allowed as an 'exception'.) It followed that large cruisers would probably be able to outrun any ship they could not outfight. However, given the engine technology of the time, it would be very difficult to provide much armour on even 10,000 tons standard displacement if high speed (about 33 knots) was to be attained.

This and other treaties of the period also reflected the deep horror with which the sea powers viewed submarine warfare as practised by Germany during World War I. Even so, attempts at Washington and elsewhere to ban submarines failed. Navies found them too useful, for example, as a means of attacking warships inside areas controlled by enemy surface forces. Submarines were also seen as ideal scouts in such areas, as indeed was to be proved during World War II.

By 1922 several navies had aircraft carriers, either built from scratch or converted from cruisers. It was clear that the carrier had an important future, but just how important no one could say. The number and total tonnage of carriers were limited according to the 5:5:3 ratio for battleships, and special treaty provisions permitted the conversion into carriers of a specific number of battleships or battlecruisers otherwise scheduled for scrapping. This was the origin of the U.S. *Lexington* and *Saratoga*, the Japanese *Kaga* and *Akagi*, the British

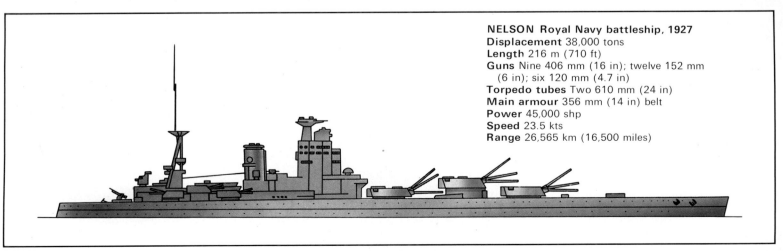

NELSON Royal Navy battleship, 1927
Displacement 38,000 tons
Length 216 m (710 ft)
Guns Nine 406 mm (16 in); twelve 152 mm (6 in); six 120 mm (4.7 in)
Torpedo tubes Two 610 mm (24 in)
Main armour 356 mm (14 in) belt
Power 45,000 shp
Speed 23.5 kts
Range 26,565 km (16,500 miles)

Courageous and *Glorious*, and the French *Béarn*. Carrier aircraft were relatively inexpensive, and even the smaller 'flat-tops' could accommodate them in large numbers. Both Japan and the United States began, in the mid-1920s, to look toward carrier aircraft as a means of getting around the limits on naval power imposed at Washington. One element in this thinking was that, with battleships limited in number and very difficult to replace in wartime, it would be impossible to subject the battle fleets to many risks. Both the United States and Japan expected a future war to culminate in a major fleet engagement, a kind of super-Jutland, in the western Pacific, probably near the Philippines or in Japanese home waters. However, before such a battle there would be a long period of commerce raiding and probably U.S. offensive operations to seize bases in those areas. Neither side would be eager to risk its few battleships in such operations, but the lighter-built carriers would be easier to replace. In fact, both navies developed plans to convert fast merchant ships into auxiliary aircraft carriers in an emergency.

As aircraft developed, both navies came to see in carriers an important strike force and, indeed, some officers had already begun to envisage the carrier as a replacement for the battleship as a fleet's main striking unit. But it must be remembered that the wood-and-canvas airplanes of the 1920s and early 1930s lacked the speed, range, weapon capacity, and even navigational instruments effectively to challenge modern warships underway.

The Royal Navy did not hold so radical a view, largely because it did not operate its own aircraft. With the establishment of the independent Royal Air Force in 1918, naval aircraft on British carriers had become the property – in many ways the neglected stepchild – of the Royal Air Force. This situation was remedied only in 1937, after most of the decisions concerning British naval air programmes for the next few years had already been made.

Thus, in the aftermath of the wholesale limitation of battle fleets at Washington, most navies were still able to build significant cruiser and carrier forces. The speed and seakeeping ability of both made them an ideal combination for independent operations, at least in the American and Japanese navies. All navies were left with battle fleets consisting mostly of ships designed before 1914 and so not incorporating wartime advances in anti-torpedo construction. Under the treaty they could be (and many were) rebuilt with 'blisters' for underwater protection and with extra deck armour against bombing and long-range gunfire. Such reconstruction, however, could not redress the chief deficiency of the existing ships – their low speed compared with the new generation of carriers and large cruisers. This speed problem alone made tactical combination of battleships and carriers

A Martin T4M torpedo-bomber, with arrester-hook lowered, prepares to land aboard the giant carrier USS *Saratoga* in 1937. The *Saratoga* and her sister, the *Lexington*, were conversions of battlecruiser designs and were completed in 1927. Until the *Essex*-class entered service in 1943 onwards they were the largest carriers in the world, displacing 39,000 tons and with a length of 253 m (830 ft). The *Saratoga* carried 80 aircraft. Visible in the photograph are two of the *Saratoga*'s four twin turrets which carried 203 mm (8 in) guns fore and aft of the island; they were removed before the United States entered the war.

Inset The *Deutschland* (1933), first of the German 'pocket battleships' (large armoured cruisers) to be completed.

difficult, and so encouraged independent-minded carrier commanders. (Lighter and more powerful engines, developed between the wars partly as a result of the need to build treaty cruisers with better protection, would make possible the construction of fast battleships able to operate with carriers and yet conform to treaty limits; these ships appeared in all major navies from the mid-1930s onwards. By then, of course, navies with fast carriers had learnt how to operate carrier task forces.)

By the late 1920s a building race in fast cruisers had developed between Britain, Japan, and the United States, and to a lesser degree between France and Italy. Once again there were warnings that the naval arms race might lead to war; moreover, the participants were sobered by the deepening world depression. So in 1930 a new naval-arms-limitation conference was convened in London, one of its tasks being to consider an extension of the 10-year battle-ship-building moratorium agreed upon at Washington eight years before. Japan protested against its 'short end' of the 5:5:3 ratio, and when new limits on heavy cruisers were worked out at the 1930 conference Japan obtained a higher limit, although not full parity.

Her navy, although operating a large naval air arm, remained dominated by exponents of the battle line, who felt that the 5:3 edge granted the Americans by treaty would be fatal in war. Japanese defence planning began to turn on weapons not limited by treaty: destroyers and cruisers fitted with the huge 610 mm (24 in) diameter 'Long Lance' torpedoes; seaplanes based in island groups through which the U.S. fleet would have to pass; and submarines, both very large and midget. There was increasing pressure in Japan to renounce (or at least to flout) the treaties; many Japanese strategists felt that, if they were able to build in total secrecy, they could construct battleships so powerful that the United States would be unable to provide effective answers in time. In fact, the Japanese formally rejected the treaties in 1936, and by March 1937 plans were approved for the construction of four super-battleships capable of overpowering any ships that the United States could build within the limitations imposed by the 33.5 m (110 ft) width of the Panama Canal locks (America's 'door' between Atlantic and Pacific). Two of these ships were constructed, the *Yamato* and *Musashi*. With a displacement of 72,809 tons and a main armament of nine 460 mm (18.1 in) guns, they were the largest and most powerful battleships ever built. A third sister ship was converted during construction into the carrier *Shinano*.

The Japanese giants were only one example of attempts to achieve superiority in a world of very few battleships. In 1919 Germany had been virtually disarmed at sea; she was reduced to a few obsolete battleships, small cruisers, and torpedo boats; submarines had been prohibited entirely. By 1928, when enough money had become available to replace the existing battle-ships, the German naval staff looked to some-thing quite new – very fast *Panzerschiffe* (arm-oured cruisers) capable of extreme cruising range thanks to diesel engines. There was no equivalent to these 'pocket battleships' in any other navy: the Washington Treaty forbade construction of cruisers with battleship guns – the German ships were to have six 280 mm (11 in) guns – and in a world of few battleships there seemed little point in wasting scarce tonnage or capital on specialised commerce raiders.

The Arms Race Quickens

When the German plans were announced they caused particular alarm in the French Navy, which had been considering something on roughly the same lines for several years. France had been permitted to build a new battleship to replace the *France*, lost by grounding in 1922. In 1932 she laid down a fast battlecruiser, the *Dunkerque*, and so initiated a new European battleship-building race. The *Dunkerque*, with more than twice the displacement of the German 15,900-ton *Deutschland* of 1929 (and her later sisters *Admiral Scheer* and *Admiral Graf Spee*), was the minimum counter to the *Panzerschiffe* with which French naval officers could feel comfortable. She had to be well enough armoured to resist German shellfire, fast enough to run down the German ships, and powerful enough to destroy them rapidly at very long range. However, the *Dunkerque* was herself faster, at 30 knots, than any ship which outgunned her except HMS *Hood*. Long before her completion, the Italians, traditional rivals of the French, laid down their own reply, a full-sized (indeed, over-sized) battleship, the 45,750-ton *Littorio* with nine 381 mm (15 in) guns, and with a similar speed.

The *Littorio* and her sister *Vittorio Veneto* were laid down in October 1934, on the eve of a conference due to review the treaty situation. (On the other side of the world Japan was already covertly withdrawing from the entire treaty structure and refusing to disclose her building plans.) Although the new London Treaty of 1935 retained limits on battleship size and firepower, it was no longer possible to prohibit new construction, or indeed even to limit total numbers, and the new naval arms race was soon in full swing. It was abetted rather than curbed by the Anglo-German agreement of 1935, which permitted Germany to begin building full-size capital ships, including the 50,150-ton *Bismarck* and her sister the *Tirpitz*, both laid down in 1936.

As the Japanese had noted, in a world of laws the lawbreaker enjoys considerable advantages: no one wanted to dissolve the treaty structure over charges of cheating on indi-vidual ships; yet from the early 1930s Japan and Italy deliberately lied about the tonnages of their new cruisers in order to conceal their power. The other governments proved remark-ably credulous. For example, when an Italian heavy cruiser of the *Zara* class was damaged in a collision in the Mediterranean, she had to be dry-docked at Gibraltar under the eyes of the Royal Navy – who soon saw that she displaced over 13,000 tons rather than the 10,000 permit-ted by treaty. (The official British reaction was that 'some navies find it difficult to keep within designed weights' – in other words, the extra 3,000 tons was really a measure of Italian incompetence in shipbuilding rather than of deliberately applied extra armour and horse-power.) These practices extended to the German Navy even before the rise of Hitler in 1933, and

they were continued as the new Italian, German, and Japanese battleships were built. For example, both the *Littorio* and the *Bismarck* were actually some 7,000 tons heavier than announced, and the vast, ultra-secret *Yamatos*, of course, were never announced at all.

Germany had been denied submarines by the Versailles Treaty of 1919, but the former U-boat men were well aware of what they might achieve in a future war. A German design bureau was set up in the Netherlands, and prototypes for future U-boats were designed and built for other navies, including the new Soviet fleet. When Hitler came to power the designers returned to Germany and new U-boats were laid down, an arrangement formally acknowledged in the 1935 Anglo-German Treaty. Fortunately for the Allies, the German Navy (and Hitler himself) for long remained obsessed with surface sea power: when war broke out in 1939 there were only 57 German submarines.

The Royal Navy concentrated before World War II on the menace presented by the armed surface ship. In wartime it would be very difficult to provide enough cruisers to protect the vast British seaborne trade. As for submarines, the British believed that they held the answer in asdic (named after the Allied Submarine Detection Investigation Committee of 1917). This acoustic detection device, developed at the end of World War I, projects a sharp 'ping' of sound that is reflected from a submerged object, such as a submarine. At first asdic seemed to eliminate the submarine's chief asset,

its invisibility. Experience would show, however, that that was far from enough. Asdic had a relatively short range, about 2,000 m at most, and searched very slowly, so that it was quite easy for a submarine to penetrate an asdic 'screen' around a convoy. It proved best for maintaining contact with a submarine already detected – that is, a submarine which had announced its presence by the visible track of its torpedoes. Then asdic could permit a hunting ship to stay with the submarine and to drop patterns of depth charges (underwater bombs). The Germans found, however, that at night their submarines were virtually invisible when on the surface – undetectable by asdic and difficult to spot by early versions of radar (radio detection and ranging).

The British, not suspecting the magnitude of the problem they would soon face, could not afford to invest heavily in small anti-submarine craft, which would be extremely expensive to man. Believing that surface raiders would be the chief threat to their trade in wartime, they invested most of their naval budget in cruisers and in modernisation of the battle fleet with which they would try to maintain control of the North Atlantic and the Mediterranean. In the latter sea they had to face not merely a potentially hostile Italian fleet but also a large land-based Italian air force and a large and well-advertised force of Italian motor torpedo boats. It was assumed, however, that the French Navy would share the British burden in the Mediterranean.

The war against China during the late 1930s gave Japan an opportunity to gain combat experience in the use of carrier forces. Here the carrier *Kaga* (26,900 tons) prepares to launch some of her 60 aircraft during manoeuvres off southern Japan in May 1937, two months before the war flared into major conflict.

45

CHAPTER 6
WAR IN THE ATLANTIC

Preceding two pages
Battle of the River Plate: the British cruisers *Ajax* and *Achilles* (7,260 tons) engage the *Admiral Graf Spee* on 13 December 1939. With the larger *Exeter* (8,250 tons), the British cruisers forced the heavier-gunned armoured cruiser to put into Montevideo for repairs. Four days later the *Graf Spee* was scuttled in the River Plate estuary on Hitler's orders.

The 38,900-ton battleship *Scharnhorst*, completed in 1939, and her sister ship *Gneisenau* were the largest German warships operational when the war began. Although capable of 32 kts, their nine 11 in (280 mm) guns in triple turrets and relatively light horizontal protection made them more effective as commerce raiders than as battleships. The *Scharnhorst* was sunk off the North Cape (Norway) by HMS *Duke of York* in December 1943.

World War II began as a land war with the German invasion of Poland on 1 September 1939, but it was soon transformed into a land and naval war as Britain and France attempted to come to the assistance of Poland. They could not slow the German *Blitzkrieg*, but they did declare a blockade of Germany similar to that which had proved so effective a quarter of a century earlier. In reply the Germans began unrestricted submarine warfare; the first victim was the British liner *Athenia*, sunk on 3 September – and a further 40 merchant vessels were destroyed that month. So too was the aircraft carrier HMS *Courageous*, sunk while on anti-submarine patrol in the Western Approaches to the English Channel by the *U-29*. Then on 14 October, the *U.47* struck a deadly blow against British morale by sailing into the waters of the Home Fleet's base at Scapa Flow, in Orkney, and sinking the obsolescent 27,500-ton battleship *Royal Oak*.

Early Engagements
These were mainly isolated incidents, however: the European naval war truly got underway with German submarines and surface raiders in the Atlantic, originally as a precaution against the possibility that the invasion of Poland might bring Britain and France into the war. (Hitler had expected his Polish conquest to proceed without British and French intervention, and the German Navy did not expect to have to face the major sea powers until after it had completed its long-range building programme, the 'Z-plan', in about 1946). The German Navy had three pocket battleships of around 16,000 tons, two standard battleships (*Scharnhorst* and *Gneisenau*) of 38,900 tons, two heavy cruisers (*Hipper* class) of 18,400 tons, and a variety of lesser craft in commission; under construction were three more heavy cruisers, two battleships, and two aircraft carriers, and much more had been authorised. Of all these ships, only the two battleships (*Bismarck* and *Tirpitz* of 50,150 tons) and one heavy cruiser would be completed. Until well into 1942 Hitler

refused to accept that the war would be a lengthy one, and was unwilling to invest in ships which could not be completed rapidly.

In this early phase of the war German submarines had to travel a considerable distance before they could reach the open Atlantic, and so they could not remain on patrol for very long. They were not as effective as were the commerce raiders. The pocket battleship *Admiral Graf Spee*, for example, sank nine merchant ships totalling 50,000 tons on a cruise ending at Montevideo, Uruguay, in December 1939. Just as important, she tied up a large proportion of the British and French fleets which had to hunt her down. The Germans concluded that if ever they could get enough such raiders to sea, the enemy fleets would would be so occupied that at least some of the raiders would be able to operate almost unhindered.

In fact the *Graf Spee* was ultimately tracked down by three small British cruisers – HMS *Exeter* (8,250 tons), with six 203 mm (8 in) guns, and the sister ships *Ajax* and *Achilles* (7,260 tons), with eight 152 mm (6 in) guns – which in theory should have proved easy meat for the powerful 280 mm (11 in) guns of the German ship at long range. In fact, the *Graf Spee*'s diesel engines made her a good 6 knots slower than the British ships, which were thus able to bring their lighter guns into effective range. Although *Exeter* was severely damaged in the battle, she scored sufficient hits on the *Graf Spee* to oblige the latter to put into the neutral harbour of Montevideo for repairs. These delayed her long enough for the Allies, by a series of diplomatic deceptions, to convince the Germans that the British and French had concentrated battleships and even an aircraft carrier off Montevideo. The Germans decided that it was better to destroy their ship than to allow her to be sunk in battle, and on 17 December Captain Hans Langsdorff scuttled the *Graf Spee* off Montevideo, and then shot himself.

The war on land was soon to provide the Germans with a much better system of bases for submarine warfare against Britain. After a winter of inactivity on land (the Phoney War), Germany invaded Norway and Denmark in April 1940. The British and French navies landed allied troops in Norway, and in fact the German Navy suffered badly as it attempted to support its invasion. One German heavy cruiser, the *Blücher*, fell victim to a torpedo launched by an old Norwegian coastal fortification. German destroyers were sunk by a British force of destroyers backed by the battleship *Warspite*, and the German light cruiser *Königsberg* was sunk at Bergen by British naval dive-bombers from Orkney – the first major fighting ship to be sunk by aircraft in a war. At about the same time her sistership *Karlsruhe* was fatally damaged by the British submarine *Truant*. However, on land the Germans soon gained the upper hand, due in large part to their successful integration of troops, tanks, and tactical aircraft, particularly the Junkers Ju 87D Stuka dive-bomber. The Stukas were able to inflict terrible losses on the ships supporting Allied troops at Narvik; while the battleships *Scharnhorst* and *Gneisenau* sank the aircraft carrier HMS *Glorious* during the British withdrawal.

The U-boat Campaign

By now the German surface fleet was badly reduced, with many of its ships in dockyard for repairs following damage off Norway. However, the German Army, largely intact after the Norwegian campaign, was advancing rapidly through the Low Countries and France. This was a land campaign with important naval consequences. In World War I German bases in Belgium had contributed notably to the submarine campaign against Britain because they permitted U-boats to be based close to the British trade routes. With the fall of France in the summer of 1940 Germany could, potentially at least, base her U-boats on a vast stretch of the Atlantic seaboard from Norway to the Spanish frontier of France. The French bases, especially, were greatly to advance the cause of the German U-boat and commerce-raider campaigns in the Atlantic, since these vessels could now avoid the hazardous passage through the Strait of Dover or around the northern coast of Scotland. Through these land victories, then, the German U-boat fleet became a menace throughout the Atlantic Ocean. Its operations were greatly extended by the use of special supply U-boats ('Milch Cows') that could refuel other submarines in mid-ocean.

Churchill would later write that the U-boat war alone caused him continuous anxiety between 1940 and 1945; every other menace he could overcome, but this one he knew could defeat Britain: 'The U-boat was our worst evil. It would have been wise for the Germans to stake all upon it.' Nor were the prospects bright for effective anti-submarine warfare (ASW). Pre-war economies and the misplaced faith in asdic meant that few escort vessels were available in 1940 and 1941. Although defensive convoys were soon instituted, the German submarines began to attack in wolf-packs, overwhelming the convoy escorts. Moreover, the Germans succeeded in breaking the British convoy-radio codes, so that they could often discover British plans to evade known concentrations of U-boats and plan their operations accordingly. It was clear even in 1940 that a combination of vast numbers of escorts and aircraft (to keep the U-boats submerged, and so slow them down, as well as to kill them) would be required, but these did not become available until 1943. Although by that time considerable technical improvements (such as sea-search radar) had also been applied to the U-boat war, it was probably the sheer numbers of ASW ships and aircraft that ultimately proved decisive. The present commander-in-chief of the Soviet Navy, Admiral Sergei G. Gorshkov, has observed that 'for each German U-boat there were 25 British and U.S. warships and 100 aircraft, and for every German submariner at sea there were one hundred British and American anti-submariners. A total of six million men was thrown into the anti-submarine war'.

The fall of France had two other important effects on the Atlantic battle. First, it removed from the Allied side the fourth most powerful navy in the world. Although many French units fled across the Mediterranean to the French colonies in Africa, Churchill feared that they would ultimately be handed over to the Germans as part of a peace settlement. He ordered British admirals at Oran (Algeria) and Alexandria (Egypt) to offer the French fleets in those two ports a choice: to be disarmed or to join the Allies. At Oran the French admiral refused to choose and a British force attacked him at anchor, sinking one French battleship with great loss of life. The remainder of the French force in Oran returned to the main French base at Toulon, in a portion of France which the Germans had agreed not to occupy. Meanwhile, at Alexandria cooler heads prevailed and the French commander agreed to remain in the harbour as a neutral. (His ships would make up the kernel of the Free French Navy that was to be formed in 1943.)

Upper The Type 7B *U-47* honoured at Kiel by the crew of the light cruiser *Emden*. Commanded by Gunther Prien, she sank the battleship *Royal Oak* in the waters of Scapa Flow in October 1939.

Lower A British poster stressing the importance of keeping the movements of convoy ships secret.

A careless word...

...A NEEDLESS SINKING

The Mediterranean Theatre

The second major consequence of the defeat of France was the intervention of Italy. In June 1940, seeing his old enemy France nearly prostrate, Mussolini declared war and invaded along the French Riviera. A desert war in North Africa now began between British troops based originally in Egypt and the Italians (later reinforced by the Germans) in Libya. It would seesaw back and forth until the Battle of El Alamein, in the summer of 1943, opened the decisive Allied westward advance along the North Africa coast.

The Italian Navy possessed a force of very fast, modern battleships, which the Royal Navy could not match without weakening its fleet in the Atlantic. The British Admiralty therefore planned a surprise air strike on the main fleet base at Taranto, on the 'heel' of Italy, on 10-11 November 1940. Only one British carrier, HMS *Illustrious*, was available and she could launch only 20 venerable Fairey Swordfish biplanes for the night torpedo attack, but it proved a remarkable triumph. Only two aircraft were lost in the daring raid, in which no fewer than three battleships, a cruiser, and two destroyers were crippled. Italian battleship strength was thus halved in a few hours. (The Swordfish – known generally as the 'Stringbag' – was much tougher than she looked: throughout the years 1941–3 the squadrons based on the island of Malta were to sink a monthly average of 50,000 tons of enemy shipping, some of it heavily armed.)

Nor was Taranto the only heavy blow felt by the Italians. Four months later the British Mediterranean Fleet, including the battleships *Warspite*, *Barham*, and *Valiant* and the carrier *Formidable*, caught an Italian force off Cape Matapan (on the southern tip of Greece) and in a night action sank three Italian cruisers (the sisterships *Pola*, *Zara*, and *Fiume* of 14,530 tons) and two large destroyers, while the *Formidable*'s Swordfish torpedo bombers crippled the battleship *Vittorio Veneto*. The British lost only one Swordfish in the battle. However, this by no means ended the problems of the Royal Navy in the Mediterranean. Quite soon it became obvious that the main problem there would be enemy land-based aircraft, which with the advance of the Italian and German armies into the Balkan peninsula soon came to be based along much of the northern and southern coasts of the Mediterranean.

When British forces in Greece were ejected by the Germans in the spring of 1941, they were evacuated to the island of Crete. There the Germans attacked with parachute troops. Their attempts at seaborne landings for reinforcement proved disastrous, thanks to the Royal Navy; but the latter's operations to evacuate British troops from Crete were also far from successful, and German and Italian dive bombers sank many British ships sorely needed elsewhere.

The Italian battleship *Caio Duilio* (28,918 tons) lies on the bottom in Taranto's outer harbour after being hit by a torpedo from a Fairey Swordfish in November 1940. Completed originally in 1915, she had been reconstructed in 1937–40, and had a main armament of ten 320 mm (12.6 ins) guns. After the Taranto raid she was refloated and repaired, and she re-entered service in December 1941.

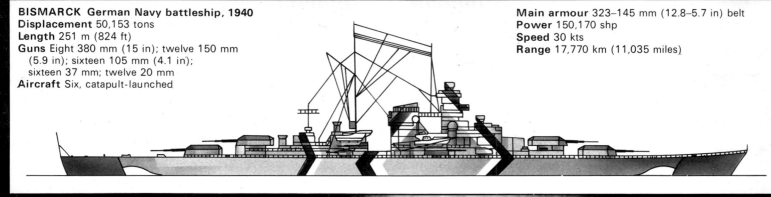

BISMARCK German Navy battleship, 1940
Displacement 50,153 tons
Length 251 m (824 ft)
Guns Eight 380 mm (15 in); twelve 150 mm
(5.9 in); sixteen 105 mm (4.1 in);
sixteen 37 mm; twelve 20 mm
Aircraft Six, catapult-launched

Main armour 323–145 mm (12.8–5.7 in) belt
Power 150,170 shp
Speed 30 kts
Range 17,770 km (11,035 miles)

The End of the Bismarck

British losses off Crete were soon felt in the Atlantic, where the programme of new U-boat construction ordered early in the war was taking effect. Moreover, since the outbreak of war the Germans had completed one battleship, the *Bismarck*, and a heavy cruiser, the *Prinz Eugen*, while the *Tirpitz*, sister to the *Bismarck*, was nearly ready. Commerce raiding by, among others, the pocket battleship *Admiral Scheer* and the larger *Scharnhorst* and *Gneisenau* had already shown how seriously the Royal Navy was likely to be stretched.

In May 1941 the Germans sent out the powerful team of the *Bismarck* and the *Prinz Eugen*. They were detected as they steamed through Swedish and Norwegian waters, and the battlecruiser *Hood*, the pride of the Royal Navy, was sent to intercept them in company with the brand new battleship *Prince of Wales* (41,000 tons) and six destroyers. The opposing forces met at dawn on 24 May in the Denmark Strait (between Greenland and Iceland). As at Jutland, German gunnery proved superior. The *Bismarck* quickly sank the too-lightly armoured *Hood*, her shells touching off a magazine explosion aft that broke the British ship in half. Only three of the *Hood's* crew of 1,419 officers and men survived the explosion. In turn, the *Prince of Wales*, also damaged, with a raw crew

and with some of her guns not yet operational, managed to secure a long-range hit on the *Bismarck* that started an oil leak. Having lost 1,000 tons of oil fuel, the *Bismarck* turned southeast, hoping to reach the French port of Brest for repairs.

The Royal Navy feverishly concentrated a vast force against the *Bismarck*. The Germans managed to evade the *Prince of Wales* and its destroyers, but in the mistaken belief that he could not lose his shadowers the German captain transmitted a long radio message to base which the British intercepted and used to locate the *Bismarck* once more. Swordfish bombers from the carrier *Ark Royal*, which had steamed northward from Gibraltar, put a torpedo into *Bismarck's* stern, jamming her rudder, so that she began to steam in large circles, only a few hundred miles from the French coast and safety. Now, however, the British battleships which had been in pursuit were able to close, and the *King George V* and *Rodney* poured shells into the German flagship. Even at relatively short range, however, the British gunnery was poor, most of the shells blasting away the superstructure well above the waterline. The cruiser *Dorsetshire* finally closed in and torpedoed the *Bismarck*; the Germans were to claim that they had scuttled her when further resistance became hopeless.

The battleship *Bismarck*, seen from the heavy cruiser *Prinz Eugen*, fires a broadside during the action against HMSS *Hood* and *Prince of Wales*. After the *Bismarck* had sunk the *Hood* with her fifth salvo, the two German ships separated, the *Prince Eugen* reaching sanctuary at Brest eight days later.

The Murmansk Convoys

The complexion of the Atlantic war changed yet again after Germany invaded its erstwhile ally, the Soviet Union, in June 1941. Now it became necessary to get war supplies to the Russians, and there were only two possible sea routes: north, around Norway to the ice-free port of Murmansk; or south, around the Cape of Good Hope (passage through the Mediterranean being unsafe at best), through the Persian Gulf to Iran, and across Iran to the Soviet Union. The southern route was relatively safe but enormously long; the northern was horrendously dangerous, given the mass of German air and submarine bases in Norway. Moreover, in the north natural hazards such as ice added considerably to those presented by the Germans. The very low temperatures of Arctic waters had unusual effects. For example, as ships pitched in heavy seas, the spray itself began to freeze, adding topweight, and also making guns and other gear inoperable unless they could be thawed by steam hoses. The delicate mechanism of torpedoes also iced up: in one action the British cruiser *Trinidad* fired a torpedo which circled back on the ship and fatally damaged her.

Behind the U-boats and torpedo bombers lay the heavy ships of the German fleet, secure in their deep-water anchorages in the Norwegian fjords. To counter this threat the British always had to have battleships available in support of their convoys. Generally, the forces directly covering the convoy were considered responsible for defence against submarines and aircraft. But they were rarely strong enough to beat off, for example, a pocket battleship. In theory that was the function of a distant covering force. The merchant ships of the convoy might scatter so as to minimize losses to the German battleship, which would then be engaged by the covering battle force. In fact these tactics were employed only once, in July 1942, when the Admiralty believed that the *Tirpitz* was about to engage convoy PQ-17. The dispersal had disastrous effects; the battleship never emerged from her base, but the merchant ships, now effectively unescorted, were easy targets for German submarines and bombers, which sank 21 vessels over five days.

This success encouraged the Germans to try other surface attacks, which generally proved far less effective. For example, on 31 December 1942 the two heavy cruisers *Admiral Hipper* and *Lützow* (ex-*Deutschland*) and six destroyers attacked convoy JW-51B, covered by four *Onslow*-class destroyers – each armed with only four 102 mm (4 in) guns – two other destroyers, and five smaller vessels. In distant cover were two British light cruisers with 152 mm (6 in) guns. The entire force should have been no match for the Germans. In fact, it proved more than adequate, the British destroyers keeping the German ships away from the convoy by the threat of attack with their torpedoes. The *Hipper* was damaged and withdrew, and one of her destroyers was sunk. This fiasco so enraged Hitler that he ordered all surviving German capital ships to be laid up as coastal-defence fortifications. The commander of the German Navy, Grand Admiral Erich Raeder, resigned in protest, and in fact the order was rescinded. Admiral Karl Dönitz, chief of the U-boat force, now became commander of the Navy – an appointment that symbolized the supreme importance of the submarine in German strategy.

German surface operations culminated in an abortive attack by the battleship *Scharnhorst* on Murmansk convoy JW-55B at the end of December 1943. By this time British code-breaking was so effective that the battleship's mission was known in detail even before she steamed out of her Norwegian base. She was caught by a British force that included the battleship *Duke of York*, four cruisers, and a number of destroyers, and was sunk by a combination of torpedoes and radar-directed salvoes from the battleship's 356 mm (14 in) guns.

The Allied convoys sailing around the North Cape to the Russian port of Murmansk were the most perilous of the war, being under constant threat of attack from German aircraft, surface warships, and submarines based in Norway. Here a freighter, carrying a balloon to deter low-level attacks by aircraft, is torpedoed by a U-boat after the disastrous scattering of convoy PQ-17 in July 1942.

Neutralising the U-boat Menace

The United States formally entered the war in December 1941. In the North Atlantic, however, U.S. warships had been involved for some months prior to that, convoying merchant vessels to Iceland and reporting any German U-boats they detected. The Germans responded to this 'unofficial' American participation by attacking U.S. escorts. During this period two U.S. destroyers were torpedoed by U-boats and one, the *Reuben James*, was sunk on 31 October 1941. From December onwards the Germans moved long-range U-boats into U.S. coastal waters and took heavy toll of the U.S. coastal tanker traffic. They were helped by the reluctance of the American seaside resorts to accept a 'blackout' even though their lights were proving extremely helpful to the U-boats. It was not until the autumn of 1942 that the U.S. Navy had enough escorts to establish coastal convoys; thereafter the U-boats withdrew into the central North Atlantic.

One important factor in the ASW campaign was the ever-increasing coverage of the North Atlantic by Allied aircraft. A submarine could make good speed (10 knots or more) only on the surface; submerged, she was in effect a manned mine capable of striking but not of moving in search of targets. A surfaced submarine, however, is easy prey for aircraft, and one of the most important effects of Allied air cover was to force down the submarines. There was, how-

ever, an air-cover gap in the middle of the North Atlantic – a strip of ocean that was beyond the effective range of American aircraft in the west, British aircraft in the east, and British aircraft based on Iceland in the north; and although this gap steadily contracted with improved aircraft performance, it for long remained a safety zone for U-boats. The Germans also employed the big Focke-Wulf Fw 200C Condor bombers to attack convoys and to provide intelligence for the U-boat command in France.

Quite early on it became clear that the best answer was aircraft carriers to accompany convoys; but carriers were few and convoys were many. The problem was answered by the escort carrier, a small flat-top converted from a merchant-ship hull. The Americans produced 116 such ships during the war and another 25 were built in Britain. Escort carriers became available in mid-1943, at about the same time as other escort ships became available in large numbers. The combination, plus the introduction of improved sonar (sound navigation and ranging) for U-boat detection and new ASW weapons such as 'Hedgehog' (a mortar for firing anti-submarine bombs) and, later, the more-powerful 'Squid', was decisive. In April and May 1943 the Germans lost 56 U-boats and sank only 92 merchant ships – a ratio so unfavourable that for a time they withdrew their submarines from the North Atlantic. The battle would never again turn in the Germans' favour.

The Atlantic battle against the U-boats turned in favour of the Allies from mid-1943. An important element in this success was the use of small escort carriers (converted merchantman), whose aircraft could hunt U-boats in mid-Atlantic areas that were beyond the range of land-based bombers. Seen here is USS *Card*, one of more than 100 such carriers produced by the United States during the war. The aircraft on the flight deck are Grumman TBF Avengers, which could carry a 559 mm (22 in) torpedo or 907 kg (2,000 lb) of bombs.

Amphibious Landing Craft

If the defence of the great routes across the Atlantic and the Mediterranean and around the North Cape was the central theme of naval warfare in the European theatre, amphibious operations also played a vital role. The first major amphibious operations of the war were the German air and naval landings in Norway in 1940 and the ill-fated British landings to counter them. After the fall of France in mid-1940 the German Army began to plan Operation Sealion, the invasion of Britain. Just how serious the plan was in Hitler's mind still is not clear, since in the light of later amphibious operations it appears ludicrous. One view is that Sealion was planned merely as a sop to Hitler; it has also been argued that Hitler allowed preparations for Sealion to go forward in order to disguise his plans for invasion of the Soviet Union. At all events, it could not have been seriously entertained unless the Germans could command the English Channel by sea and in the air.

With the Germans in control of the entire western seaboard of continental Europe north of neutral Spain, however, the British could do little more than carry out raids. In purely military terms these raids had little value (although they raised British public morale), and in most the loss of men was high. But they played an important part in the development of the techniques that would be required for the eventual invasion of Europe. The British-Canadian assault on Dieppe in 1942 was particularly valuable in this respect. By that time the United States was also in the war, and it was accepted that American industrial capacity would be required to produce the enormous number of landing craft needed. British experience in raids influenced the design of these vehicles, the most famous of which was the ocean-going Landing Ship, Tank (LST).

The landing craft had to beach themselves on a hostile shore and discharge assault troops and tanks with sufficient speed and in sufficient numbers to overcome heavily entrenched enemy defences. Although merchant ships could carry most of the invading troops and their vehicles, such vessels would have to unload lighters or small landing craft by boom from their holds – a time-consuming and exceedingly hazardous process. The LSTs, on the other hand, merely had to beach, open their enormous doors, and let the tanks drive out. There was also the LSD (Landing Ship, Dock), which could transport several loaded landing craft or amphibious tractors, and there were other craft more specialised still.

LSTs unload vehicles and supplies on a Normandy beachhead during the Allied invasion of France in June 1944. The standard LST displaced 1,625 tons, was 100 m (328 ft) long, and could make over 11 kts. Many were converted into repair ships, hospital ships, or railway ferries.

By the spring of 1943 Allied land forces were in control of North Africa. In July an enormous invasion force sailed from Egypt, Tunisia, and Algeria and swiftly conquered Sicily. Two months later the Allies crossed the Strait of Messina and invaded mainland Italy. (The Italian government soon surrendered, but German armies continued to defend much of the northern half of Italy.) In all these operations, Allied successes depended crucially upon landing craft.

Hitherto torpedo-bombers and dive-bombers had been the main threat to Allied ships in the Mediterranean, but during the Italian campaign the Germans introduced a major new weapon: the radio-guided bomb launched by bombers at high altitude. Such missiles proved an elusive target for Allied guns, and unless their carrier planes could be destroyed at long range the weapon seemed impossible to counter. It was first used against ships of the Italian fleet that were steaming from La Spezia to surrender to the Allies after the fall of the Italian government: a single guided bomb sank the new 46,215 ton battleship *Roma*. Soon afterwards the bomb was used against landing craft at Salerno (south of Naples), and also at Anzio, where an Allied force was trying to outflank the German defensive line.

Ultimately there were two countermeasures. The first was to use radio signals to jam the radio link between the carrier aircraft and the missile, so that the latter could not be guided onto its target. This was difficult, but an effective technique was gradually devised, and jamming was certainly responsible in part for the defeat of the German guided missiles in the Mediterranean. There were also attacks on the bombers themselves, mainly at their airfields. In one such raid all the specially modified bombers in one guided-missile programme were destroyed. By that time there were not the resources to build up replacements, and the Germans abandoned the weapon. Given the concentration of shipping at the Normandy invasion a few months later, this was extremely fortunate for the Allies.

After the Anzio assault in January 1944, all available landing craft were concentrated in England for the D-Day invasion of Normandy. The mass of equipment to be unloaded here quite dwarfed the capacity of specialized craft, and it became necessary for the Allies to build an artificial harbour, code-named Mulberry, in which conventional cargo ships could be unloaded. Normandy was the greatest amphibious operation in history, and the last one on a major scale in the European phase of the war.

U-boats: the Later Technology

By this time the Germans had made several attempts to redress the balance of the submarine war. Although they were unable to do so, their innovations formed the basis of much post-war submarine development in the Soviet Union as well as in the West. The first major innovation was actually of Dutch origin: the *schnorkel*, a long, vertical pipe through which a submarine's diesel engine can 'breathe' while the craft remains submerged at periscope depth. Submerged submarines operated on storage batteries, which gave them a very limited endurance, particularly at high speed. Batteries had to be recharged regularly by means of the diesel engine – and to do this the submarine had to come to the surface. With the schnorkel, it could run submerged on its diesel. The schnorkel 'head' presented a very small radar target and so made detection by aircraft or by ships extremely difficult.

The schnorkel, however, could not by itself solve the prime source of danger to the U-boats: limited battery endurance. Once a U-boat had carried out its attack, the ASW ships would attempt to pursue and attack it, and the U-boat would have to dive deep and take evasive action at high speed. The greater that speed and the longer it could be sustained, the better the U-

Right The schnorkel air intake (on the left) enabled a submarine to charge its batteries without surfacing.

Below Two U-boats under attack by a Grumman TBF Avenger from the USS *Card* in August 1943. This explosion sank the *U-117*, a 'milch-cow' (supply boat). The *U-66*, on the left, escaped but was sunk the following year.

boat's chance of escape. Although submerged speeds of 14 or 15 kts do not seem impressive compared to the 20 kts of which ASW frigates were capable, in normal North Atlantic seas the frigates' speeds were often reduced to 10 kts or even less, whereas the submerged submarine would not be affected by wave motion. In an attempt to improve underwater speed and endurance the Germans introduced the Type XXI, the 'electric U-boat,' in which the lower half of its special double hull was almost entirely filled with batteries. The hull shape was designed for high underwater performance – its submerged top speed of 16 kts being better than its surface speed. Much was hoped for from the new sub; fortunately for the Allies, production problems slowed the massive Type XXI building programme and few saw active service.

Although the Type XXI was an enormous improvement over previous submarines, it still had an underwater range at top speed of little more than one hour. An alternative means of underwater propulsion was developed by Professor Helmuth Walter, who used hydrogen peroxide (H_2O_2) to generate steam to power a turbine engine. Potentially, at least, such an engine would enable a submarine to sustain high submerged speeds for as long as 10 hours at a time. Walter built a series of experimental boats, but no operational ones. (After the war some of his engines were captured by the Russians, while the experimental boats fell into American and British hands. All saw the Walter boat as the submarine of the future – a most formidable opponent capable of outrunning escort ships.)

The Germans also made great efforts in torpedo development, producing one which could home on the sound of an escort ship's propellers. Although countermeasures were soon developed, this torpedo was the forerunner of modern acoustic homing torpedoes. At about the same time the Americans and the British introduced their own homing torpedo, an aircraft-launched device that had some success against U-boats. Another German invention was the pattern-making torpedo, which was programmed to change course so that it cruised to and fro across the columns of a convoy until it struck a target. The virtue of such a weapon was that it could be fired at long range, so that the submarine had a much better chance of evading the convoy escort. Such torpedoes, too, are a staple weapon of the modern submarine.

With these and other innovations the destructive potential of the U-boat forces was vastly increased. That their success was limited was due more to the accelerating industrial breakdown of a Germany nearing military collapse than to Allied ASW techniques. Indeed, the main lesson of the Battle of the Atlantic was how close-run a thing it had been at the very end. About 100 Type XXI U-boats were being fitted out when the war ended, and by then the Allied navies were firmly convinced that a new revolution in ASW technology would be required if Type XXI and Walter submarines were to be defeated in any future battle of the Atlantic. Indeed, this conviction shaped their building programmes for the first decade and a half after the war, and its consequences remain evident in Western navies.

WORLD WAR II SUBMARINE CAMPAIGN

Merchant Losses to German U-Boats
(Includes Allied and Neutral Ships)

1939 (4 months)	1940	1941	1942	1943	1944	1945 (5 months)
95	822	1141	1570	597	205	97

German U-Boats Lost*

1939 (4 months)	1940	1941	1942	1943	1944	1945 (5 months)
9	22	35	86	237	241	153

* Includes three U-boats captured by the U.S. and Royal navies. At the end of the war 215 U-boats were scuttled and 154 were surrendered to the Allies.

CHAPTER 7
WAR IN THE PACIFIC

The Pacific war was above all a war of fast-carrier task forces and of amphibious assaults. It began and ended with combinations of the two. Although Japanese naval theory was founded on the assumed primacy of the battleship, Japan built up a powerful force of attack carriers during the inter-war period and developed a body of doctrine for their combined operation. Moreover, the carriers were both powerful enough to do great damage and considered sufficiently expendable to be risked in distant offensive operations.

Japan's primary aim was to conquer the 'South Seas', the Malayan Peninsula, and the Dutch East Indies (now Indonesia) to obtain raw materials. The Japanese had been fighting in China since 1937, and were becoming increasingly dependent upon overseas resources. In July 1941 they conquered Indo-China (then mainly a French possession). The Allies tried to halt Japanese aggression by cutting off supplies of oil and scrap metals. Such economic pressure was unacceptable, and Japan planned to seize the resources. To secure her flanks she would have to seize the Philippines as well.

By 1941 the Royal Navy was too badly stretched in European waters to constitute a threat to Japanese expansion, but the United States had only a fraction of her naval strength in the Atlantic, and the battleship-oriented Japanese naval leadership initially saw elimination of U.S. battleships as the key to free operations in the South Pacific.

These operations would be screened by heavy cruisers and by land-based naval aircraft, the latter flying from Indo-China and from Formosa (Taiwan). Such operations were practicable partly because of the long range built into their naval aircraft, and partly because of the experience in amphibious warfare that the Japanese Navy had acquired in its China campaign. Indeed, Japan developed her own Landing Ship,

Dock well before the Western equivalent was conceived. She also developed float-plane fighters to support landing operations.

Japan began the Pacific war with the world's best torpedo, the 610 mm (24 in) 'Long Lance', and also with great superiority in night operations, the fruit of intensive and realistic combat training before the war. Her main – and, in the end, crucial – weaknesses were a lack of shipbuilding capacity to replace lost vessels, and an underdeveloped electronics industry (a vital drawback in a war that would be fought with radar almost from the start).

Her main adversary, the United States, had an immense industrial capacity but in 1941 was only beginning to mobilize it. The U.S. Navy had long trained for carrier warfare, but its carrier aircraft were inferior to those of the Japanese. In particular, the Americans had no carrier fighter to compare with the Mitsubishi A6M Zero-Sen until the delivery of the Grumman F6F Hellcat in the spring of 1943, nor a dive-bomber more successful than the Aichi D3A ('Val') until the Douglas SBD Dauntless became available in large numbers early in 1942. Perhaps the greatest weakness of the U.S. Navy was its lack of an efficient torpedo. Great efforts had been expended in the design of a magnetic exploder which would detonate a torpedo under the keel of its target, but in fact the detonator was defective. For this reason the aggressiveness of U.S. submarine and destroyer commanders would go unrewarded for the most part until 1943. This was particularly unfortunate in that the United States had built up a large force of excellent 'fleet' (long-range) submarines before the war, partly on the theory that they would be able to help in the defence of the Philippines. The early destruction of the Japanese merchant fleet by U.S. submarines could have had fatal consequences for Japan's war effort long before 1945.

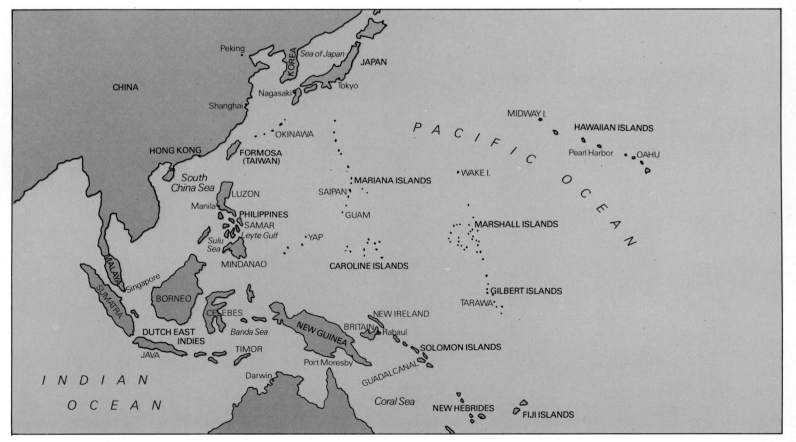

The First Engagements

Japan struck simultaneously at Pearl Harbor (Hawaii) and in the South Seas in December 1941. A scratch American-British-Dutch-Australian force of cruisers and destroyers (the ABDA force) proved completely ineffective against Japanese cruisers and destroyers escorting the troop convoys south, and twin-engined Mitsubishi G4M ('Betty') land-based naval torpedo-bombers had little difficulty in sinking two British capital ships off Malaya, the battleship *Prince of Wales* and the battle-cruiser *Repulse*, which had been rushed to the defence of Singapore.

Three days before, on 7 December, the attack on the American base at Pearl Harbor had brought the United States into the Pacific war. The attack was made from Vice-Admiral Chuichi Nagumo's task force of six aircraft carriers steaming some 320 km (200 miles) north of the Hawaiian Islands. At a cost of 27 aircraft, the attack sank four battleships, three destroyers, and one minelayer, and damaged four battleships and two cruisers. It also destroyed 188 shore-based aircraft, and killed over 2,000 sailors and soldiers. The Japanese hailed the attack as a major victory; it was indeed a triumph of planning and execution, and it dealt a devastating blow to American morale. In hindsight, however, it is clear that the Japanese success was less than it might have been. The battleships lost were all obsolescent, and the bombs and torpedoes failed to do serious damage to the port facilities or to the oil-fuel storage installations. Above all, however, was the fact that the Japanese attack had come when not a single American carrier was in port.

Thus, when two U.S. carriers returned to Pearl Harbor shortly after the attack, they were able to re-fuel and then steam out with an escort of destroyers and heavy cruisers. Given the offensive role originally ordained for the carrier-cruiser groups, the loss of the battle fleet was not nearly so serious a blow as it appeared at the time. The carriers began a series of raids on Japanese-held islands which led to the development of the tactics which would be employed throughout the war.

Meanwhile, Nagumo's fast-carrier force had turned south-westward and eventually passed into the Indian Ocean, where it began its own raids. It penetrated as far west as Ceylon, sinking the small British carrier *Hermes* and the heavy cruisers *Cornwall* and *Dorsetshire*, and later bombed installations and bases in northern Australia.

In April 1942 the U.S. carrier *Hornet* flew off 16 North American B-25 Mitchell bombers to attack Tokyo. This raid had little material effect, but it boosted American morale, as it showed that the Japanese, who until that point had been completely victorious, could themselves be struck. It prompted the Japanese to seek a wider defensive perimeter than had previously been envisaged, and thus to attempt to capture Midway Island in the Hawaiian chain. In addition, it reinforced the desire of their naval commander-in-chief, Admiral Isoroku Yamamoto, to force a decisive fleet engagement upon the U.S. Navy.

Part of the Japanese six-carrier First Air Fleet *en route* to Pearl Harbor in December 1941. In the foreground are Aichi D3A 'Val' dive-bombers aboard the 71-plane *Soryu* (18,800 tons), which was later sunk at the Battle of Midway. In the background is her sister ship the *Hiryu* (20,250 tons), distinguished by having her island superstructure on the port side; she was sunk the day after the *Soryu*.

Coral Sea and Midway

The Japanese continued to expand to the south, and on 5 May 1942 engaged a U.S. carrier force in the Battle of the Coral Sea (between the Solomon Islands and the north-east coast of Australia). This was the first engagement in history in which warships attacked each other far beyond the range of their guns, using only their aircraft. The Japanese light carrier *Shoho* and the large U.S. carrier *Lexington* (39,000 tons) were sunk. Perhaps more important, the large Japanese carrier *Shokaku* (25,675 tons) was too badly damaged to take part in the subsequent Midway operation, whereas it proved possible to refit the damaged U.S. carrier *Yorktown* (25,500 tons) in time. Moreover, the Japanese expansion southward, which was to have been continued by means of a landing at Port Moresby (New Guinea), was at last halted.

The Battle of Midway on 3 June can be seen in retrospect as the single most decisive carrier battle of the war. It was planned by Admiral Yamamoto, who had also planned the Pearl Harbor raid, and involved a rather complex series of movements: the Japanese fast carriers were to raid Midway in preparation for the slower advance of the Main Body, which included the Japanese battle line. At the same time, a landing in the Aleutian Islands in the North Pacific was planned to draw off U.S. forces, and it was hoped that the U.S. carrier force would be lured into a trap. However, American success in code-breaking provided the U.S. Navy with good indications of the elaborate Japanese plan – not that knowledge of Japanese intentions was alone sufficient to ensure victory for Yamamoto's counterpart, Admiral Chester W. Nimitz. The Japanese had four carriers at Midway under Vice-Admiral Nagumo, supported by smaller flat-tops, 11 battleships, a larger number of cruisers and destroyers, and a screen of submarines. Nimitz could assemble only three carriers, one of them

the patched-up *Yorktown*, escorted by a few cruisers and destroyers, plus a dozen submarines. But he had the advantage of knowing Japanese intentions and strength.

The Japanese carriers launched their initial strikes against Midway (not knowing that U.S. carriers were in the area) causing great damage on the island and virtually wiping out its defending aircraft. At about 07.00 hours the *Enterprise* and *Hornet* each launched one torpedo-bomber squadron, two dive-bomber squadrons, and one fighter squadron, followed about 90 minutes later by one squadron each of torpedo-bombers, dive-bombers, and fighters from the *Yorktown*. The torpedo-bombers took a dreadful hammering from Nagumo's anti-aircraft batteries and Zero-Sen fighters; they achieved no hits and 37 out of the 41 bombers were destroyed. But then came the wave of Douglas SBD dive-bombers and in a series of attacks they sank three large carriers, the *Kaga*, *Akagi*, and *Soryu*. Later, dive-bombers from the *Enterprise* and *Hornet* sank the fourth of Nagumo's large carriers, the *Hiryu*.

The American triumph was not achieved without cost, since before the *Hiryu* was destroyed her bombers had crippled the *Yorktown*, which was later sunk by a submarine. The American carrier force had numbered seven first-line ships at the start of the war. Only three – the *Saratoga*, *Enterprise*, and *Ranger* – would survive 1942; and *Ranger* (19,300 tons) was too slow and poorly armed for operations in the Pacific. However, given the United States' industrial base, which was vastly greater than that of her enemy, the Battle of Midway was an enormously significant disaster for the Japanese. The Americans had embarked on a massive programme of naval construction in 1940, and within a few months of Midway the first of the new escort carriers were becoming available to supplement the fleet carriers in amphibious and ASW operations.

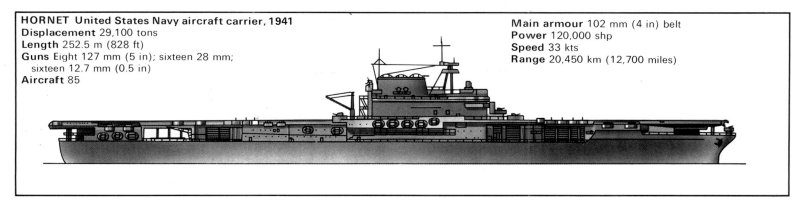

HORNET United States Navy aircraft carrier, 1941
Displacement 29,100 tons
Length 252.5 m (828 ft)
Guns Eight 127 mm (5 in); sixteen 28 mm;
   sixteen 12.7 mm (0.5 in)
Aircraft 85

Main armour 102 mm (4 in) belt
Power 120,000 shp
Speed 33 kts
Range 20,450 km (12,700 miles)

The American Counter-offensive

Meanwhile, in August 1942 the United States began its amphibious counter-offensive, landing troops on Guadalcanal in the Solomon Islands soon after the Japanese had begun to establish themselves on the island. In the restricted waters around Guadalcanal the Japanese cruisers and destroyers were able to move at night without fear of interception by U.S. carrier or land-based aircraft, and U.S. radar was not yet good enough to make up for Japanese excellence in night training. In one terrible night off Savo Island (north of Guadalcanal) the Japanese were able to sink one Australian and three U.S. heavy cruisers without loss to themselves through a combination of gunfire and the deadly 'Long Lance' heavy torpedoes.

Although the Americans finally gained naval ascendancy in the Solomons in the last months of 1942, the fierce night fighting took a terrible toll of their cruisers and destroyers. Towards the end, however, two new U.S. battleships saw successful action. In November the 406 mm (16 in) guns of the *Washington* (45,370 tons) sank the battlecruiser *Kirishima* (36,600 tons) – a victory that owed much to the growing efficiency of naval radar. In a related action the similarly armed but much more heavily armoured *South Dakota* made effective use of her advanced fire-control system and heavy anti-aircraft batteries to shoot down 26 Japanese planes in one engagement without damage to herself. The *South Dakota's* armour came through with flying colours when she survived 42 shells hits, including some from 356 mm (14 in) guns.

The *South Dakota* sustained this damage in one of the only two battleship-versus-battleship engagements of the Pacific war. By now the mantle of 'capital' ship had passed from the dreadnought to the large aircraft carrier. The older U.S. battleships were used mainly to lay down a heavy-gun barrage in support of amphibious landings. The new high-speed battleships – typified by the 33-knot *Iowa* (57,540 tons) and her sisters – were used to escort the carriers. The new battleships on both sides were equipped with a formidable array of anti-aircraft weapons. The *Iowa*, for instance, had 76 40 mm (1.6 in), 48 20 mm (0.8 in), and 20 127 mm (5 in) high-angle guns in addition to her main armament of nine 406 mm (16 in) guns. On the Japanese side the major battleships operated separately from the carriers. Even so, the gigantic *Yamato's* nine 460 mm (18.1 in) main armament was eventually backed up by 24 high-angle 127 mm (5 in) guns and no fewer than 146 25 mm (1 in) guns.

By the close of 1942 the Japanese had withdrawn their main fleet to its base at Rabaul on New Britain (immediately to the west of the Solomons), where it awaited the chance of a conclusive fleet engagement. This was not forthcoming, and for a time the Japanese Navy transferred most of the aircraft from its main carrier force to land bases in the Solomons in the hope of preventing the Allied north-westward advance through the chain of islands. In the event, most of these aircraft were destroyed in a long series of engagements during the first half of 1943. The Japanese carriers remained intact, but without their trained pilots they were impotent.

American naval strategy in the Pacific evolved into a pair of parallel advances, one island-hopping north-westward up through the Solomons and beyond, the other moving across the central Pacific supported by fast-carrier air strikes. By mid-1943 American naval construction was not merely replacing losses but expanding the U.S. carrier force considerably. An important element in this expansion was the decision, taken early in 1942, to convert nine unfinished light cruisers to small, fast, carriers – the *Independence* class of 15,100 tons, each operating 45 aircraft. All were completed within about a year, and all proved useful. At the same time, the construction of the 36,380-ton *Essex*-class fleet carriers was accelerated.

Faced with the depletion of carrier pilots, the Japanese could not seek a decisive fleet engagement during 1943. They had to be content to rebuild the carrier air groups. Meanwhile, the growing U.S. submarine fleet, its torpedo troubles largely cured, began to disrupt Japanese commerce and had considerable success against the vital Japanese oil tankers. As the advance up the Solomons continued, the Japanese fleet was forced out of Rabaul and back into home waters. Meanwhile, the American advance across the central Pacific, which had begun with an assault on the Tarawa atoll in the Gilbert Islands in November 1943, continued through the Marshall Islands to the Marianas. From here, and specifically from the air bases on the islands of Guam and Saipan (taken in July 1944), the Boeing B-29 Superfortress bombers were within striking range of Japan.

The Japanese continued to show themselves devotees of tactical complexity, as at Midway. Knowing that their carriers would probably make a poor showing against the increasingly effective U.S. carrier air groups, they evolved a tactic in which their carriers would be used as bait to draw away U.S. carriers, while a Japan-

The USS *Hornet*, completed in October 1941, was a sister ship of the earlier *Yorktown* and *Enterprise*. She had conducted trials with fully-loaded B-25 bombers two months before the Doolittle raid on Japan. Bombers from the *Hornet* and *Enterprise* sank the *Hiryu* at Midway, but in October 1942 the *Hornet* was sunk after being hit by 10 bombs and three torpedoes in the Battle of Santa Cruz, east of the Solomon Islands.

Opposite page Battle of Midway: a Japanese carrier (probably the *Hiryu*) takes evasive action under attack from U.S. Army Boeing B-17 Fortress bombers. Neither this attack nor later ones by Douglas TBD Devastator torpedo bombers damaged the Japanese ships; but shortly afterwards Douglas SBD Dauntless dive bombers sank the carriers *Kaga*, *Akagi*, and *Soryu*, and next day the *Hiryu* was sent to the bottom.

ese battle force would make for an invasion beach and destroy the relatively vulnerable shipping concentrated there. A Japanese fleet commanders' manual describing this tactic fell into U.S. hands just before the invasion of Saipan, in the central Marianas, and may well have influenced the U.S. commander, Admiral Raymond Spruance, who chose to keep his carriers near the beachhead at Saipan. One of his problems was that, in flying off their aircraft, his carriers had to run into the wind. Given the prevailing winds, that meant that they had to steam *westward*, towards Japan, and away from the beach and the firepower support of his battleships.

The Japanese had two advantages in that their carrier aircraft outranged those of the U.S. fleet and their reconnaissance proved superior. They were therefore able to engage the U.S. carriers before the latter could attack them. However, the American pilots and their Grumman F6F Hellcat fighters were by now so superior to those of the Japanese Navy that the latter stood no chance. The most celebrated aerial massacre of the Pacific war occurred on 19 June 1944 when, in what came to be known as the Marianas Turkey Shoot, the Japanese lost 219 out of 326 aircraft attacking the U.S. carriers. At the same time, American dive-bombers destroyed a further 50 land-based aircraft on neighbouring islands. At the end of the day the Americans had lost only 29 planes.

The U.S. Navy's central Pacific fast-carrier force at Majuro atoll, Gilbert Islands, in February 1944. At left is an *Independence*-class light carrier; behind her are two fast battleships. At right is the carrier *Enterprise*, and beyond her, in the centre, are four of the new *Essex*-class carriers of about 39,800 tons. By 1945 the U.S. Navy had more than 1,000 carrier-based fighters and bombers.

Inset Four of an *Essex*-class carrier's 68 quadruple 40 mm Bofors anti-aircraft guns. The dominant role of carrier-based aircraft in the Pacific war led to greatly increased anti-aircraft armaments on U.S. and Japanese ships.

Leyte Gulf

In October the two arms of the U.S. naval advance across the Pacific came together in the invasion of the Philippines at Leyte Gulf. This led to the largest naval battles in history. The main Japanese fleet was based to the south-east in the Dutch East Indies, near its source of fuel (U.S. submarine attacks had by now so badly depleted the Japanese tanker fleet that enough oil could not be had in Japan itself). The Japanese carriers were sent northward (east of the Philippines) to act as bait, while the main force sailed into the South China Sea to approach the Philippines from the south-west. One group, including the super-battleship *Yamato* and her sister *Musashi*, was to sail through the centre of the island group, then down the east coast of Samar Island, which forms the northern coast of Leyte Gulf. The other group was to take a more direct route through the Sulu Sea and make for Surigao Strait at the southern end of the gulf. The two groups were to link up in the gulf itself.

The *Yamato* force never reached the gulf. It was hounded by a series of attacks from carrier-based aircraft in the Sibuyan Sea, north-west of Samar, the culmination of which was the sinking of the *Musashi*. The group turned about and headed west. The U.S. commander, Admiral William F. Halsey, then swallowed the bait offered by the Japanese decoy carriers. He ordered the force that had sunk the *Musashi* to

sail north-eastward in pursuit of the carriers. Halsey left the strategically vital San Bernardino Strait (dividing Samar from Luzon) guarded by a lesser force, and the *Yamato* group, having turned eastward again, passed through it under cover of darkness and began to sail southwards along the east coast of Samar towards Leyte Gulf. All that now stood between it and the virtually defenceless transports and landing craft on the invasion beaches in the gulf was a force of small escort carriers intended to provide close air support and to protect the invasion shipping from submarines. They were screened by destroyers and destroyer escorts, who could oppose the Japanese battleships and cruisers only with 127 mm (5 in) guns and torpedoes. All they could do was lay a smoke-screen between the carriers and the Japanese, and then try to blunt the Japanese attack by steaming in to fire their torpedoes. The escort-carrier aircraft attacked in support, but without anti-ship bombs.

On paper the battle was lost: the Japanese, with four battleships and eight cruisers, had far too much firepower – including the *Yamato*'s fearful 460 mm (18.1 in) guns – on their side. But the spirit of the American destroyers' sailors and the carriers' pilots carried the day. The Japanese, somewhat rattled by their experiences under air attack the day before and confused by the smoke-screen, concluded that they were in fact facing the main U.S. force of fleet carriers screened by heavy cruisers. After the loss of two of their own heavy cruisers (and the sinking of three U.S. destroyers and escorts and one carrier), the Japanese turned back.

The Japanese southern force, steaming through Surigao Strait, had the odds against it: it consisted of two battleships, one heavy cruiser, and four destroyers. It ran into a large U.S. force made up, first, of 39 torpedo boats, then 11 destroyers which attacked with torpedoes, and then a battle line of six veteran battleships (some of them survivors of the Pearl Harbor attack), eight cruisers, and nine destroyers. The result was a massacre: both Japanese battleships were sunk by torpedoes, as were two of the destroyers, while the heavy cruiser was severely mauled.

As for the Japanese decoy carriers, they escaped what should have been a certain death when Halsey, notified of the action off Samar, compounded his first error by breaking off his pursuit of them in order to rush to the aid of the escort carriers. It has been convincingly argued that Halsey should have known that he could not have reached the engagement off Samar in time, although he was the victim of confused messages sent to him from Nimitz at Pearl Harbor. Moreover, in failing to press home an attack on the Japanese carriers he denied his force of new battleships a rare opportunity to exercise their heavy guns without having to withstand a similar bombardment in reply.

Upper The *Yamato* and her sister ship the *Musashi* were the largest and most powerfully armed battleships ever built. The *Yamato* was completed at Kure dockyard in December 1941, and the *Musashi* at Kawasaki in August 1942. Both were sunk by U.S. carrier bombers – the *Musashi* succumbing to 11 torpedoes and 16 bombs at Leyte Gulf, and the *Yamato* to 10 torpedoes and five bombs near Okinawa.

Lower Hundreds of American amphibious vehicles and landing craft supported by escort carriers at the invasion of Luzon, largest of the Philippine islands, in autumn 1944.

YAMATO Imperial Japanese Navy battleship, 1941
Displacement 72,809 tons
Length 263 m (863 ft)
Guns Nine 460 mm (18.1 in); twelve 155 mm (6.1 in); twelve 127 mm (5 in); twenty-four 25 mm; four 13 mm
Aircraft Six, catapult-launched
Main armour 410–100 mm (16.1–3.9 in) belt
Power 150,000 shp
Speed 27 kts
Range 11,600 km (7,200 miles)

The Kamikaze

The battles of Leyte Gulf severely depleted the Japanese fleet but did not destroy it. However, the surviving Japanese units ended up in home ports by early in 1945, from which their mobility was greatly restricted by shortage of fuel oil. On the other hand, the U.S. fleet was now operating so close to Japan and to Japanese-held islands such as Formosa as to be almost constantly within range of Japanese land-based aircraft. The Japanese were uncomfortably aware of the deficiencies of their aircraft and of their pilots. They did not have the technology to develop guided missiles, and in any case the size of the U.S. carrier fighter force made it unlikely that single bombers carrying 'stand-off' bombs would be able to survive the attack. However, there was in Japanese culture a powerful strain of self-sacrificial patriotism, of eagerness to lay down one's life in the service of the Emperor. Such feelings were exploited in the formation of the *kamikaze* unit of pilots, whose purpose was deliberately to crash bomb-loaded aircraft on American ships. The word '*kamikaze*' means 'divine wind' – an indication of the romantic mystique in which the suicidal role of these pilots was enshrouded.

The *kamikaze* were remarkably successful. In general, anti-aircraft fire at that time could not destroy incoming aircraft: its value was its ability to force a pilot to take evasive action and thus to disrupt the work of his bomb-aimer. *Kamikaze* pilots, however, could not be deflected in this way; indeed, most most of them steered in the direction of the most intensive fire. Last-moment damage to a *kamikaze* aircraft would probably not cause it to miss its target, as by then it would be on a ballistic

trajectory. A variant on the *kamikaze* theme was the rocket-propelled, manned bomb, called *Oka* (Cherry Blossom) by the Japanese and *Baka* (Fool) by the Americans. It was released by a bomber out of anti-aircraft range, and relied on its high speed for immunity to defensive guns or fighter aircraft.

Kamikazes were first used during the last stages of the battles of Leyte Gulf, but they reached their greatest effectiveness in the invasion of Okinawa (between Formosa and Japan) in April 1945, where they sank 33 U.S. ships (all destroyers or smaller vessels) and damaged several U.S. and British aircraft carriers. In an important sense they foreshadowed the effects of guided missiles employed on a large scale. The countermeasures included special radar-picket ships to warn the fleet of incoming attackers; airborne radars (developed too late, however, to see Pacific war service) to improve advanced warning of low-flying aircraft; greatly increased anti-aircraft batteries; and a much higher proportion of fighters in carrier air groups.

The *kamikaze* menace also accelerated the development of anti-aircraft missiles. Research on such missiles had been in progress for some years, and had intensified in the spring of 1944 in response to German successes with guided bombs and missiles. In December the team which had developed the American proximity fuze – which detonated a shell near an aircraft, eliminating the need for a direct hit – began work on a guided missile code named Bumblebee. However, the attempt to produce an interim weapon before the end of the war failed, and the Bumblebee story really belongs to the post-war period.

Kamikaze! A Japanese suicide pilot just misses the U.S. 'jeep' carrier *Sangamon* during an air battle in 1945.

The Final Act

After Leyte Gulf, another landing at Lingayen Gulf, on the west coast of Luzon, the largest island, consolidated the American hold on the Philippines. The fast-carrier task force now raided Tokyo, and prepared to support landings at Iwo Jima (north of the Marianas) and then at Okinawa; both islands are relatively close to Japan itself, and were important stepping-stones to the final series of landings on the mainland Japanese islands of Kyushu and Hokkaido which were scheduled for the end of 1945.

Meanwhile, the Royal Navy began to move in from the Indian Ocean, raiding the Dutch East Indies and supporting a British advance through Burma towards Malaya. Some of the amphibious landing craft released after Okinawa were used in the re-conquest of Borneo in June 1945, but no landings were made in the Dutch East Indies, partly owing to the American desire not to encourage the re-introduction of colonial rule after the war.

By this time the Japanese merchant marine had been badly damaged by U.S. submarines, which, using a mine-detecting sonar, were able to penetrate even Japanese minefields protecting the Inland Sea between Japan and Korea. However, with U.S. Army B-29 bombers operating relatively freely over Japan, another opportunity presented itself: the bombers mined Japanese territorial waters, totally paralysing even the coastal trade. This new offensive, begun in late March 1945, proved extremely effective – far more so than German attempts to do the same thing in British coastal waters in 1940. The Japanese fleet was very nearly immobilized. Indeed, it managed only one last sortie, on 6 April 1945, when the super-battleship *Yamato*, a light cruiser, and eight destroyers steamed towards the Okinawa beachhead. They carried enough fuel oil only for the outward journey, and all aboard knew that it was no more than a massive *kamikaze* attack. They were spotted by a submarine when only half way to their destination, and the following day were sent to the bottom after attacks by wave upon wave of American carrier aircraft.

By the beginning of July the Pacific war was effectively over. The remnant of the Japanese navy, immobilised by lack of fuel, lay in home ports, its only role now being to contribute to anti-aircraft defence. Land-based B-29 bombers, plus U.S. Navy bombers based on no fewer than 15 carriers, blasted Japanese industrial and naval targets almost ceaselessly. On 6 August a B-29 dropped an atomic bomb on Hiroshima, in southern Honshu, razing much of the city and taking hideous toll of human life; three days later another exploded over Nagasaki, in Kyushu. The war formally ended on 3 September 1945 – six years to the day since Britain and France had declared war on Germany.

For the navies of the world the chief lesson of the Pacific war was the supremacy of the fast-carrier task force, a fact that Japan had most fully appreciated earlier than any other country but which, in the end, she could not exploit decisively owing to her inability to replace the carriers and trained pilots she lost in combat. The advent of the atomic bomb suggested that, if the carriers could defend themselves against air attack, they might well be able to deliver nuclear attacks of their own, so that the role of navies might go beyond the traditional control of sea routes to the exercise of decisive global power from the sea. In combination with amphibious task forces, such carriers could support the seizure of distant territory inaccessible to conventional land troops. It was widely noted that none of the amphibious operations carried out by American forces in the Pacific had been repulsed, even though many had been strongly opposed by well-entrenched Japanese defenders.

An opposing view asserted that the atomic bomb made conventional naval operations obsolete. It was argued that a few bombs dropped on major cities could quickly end a war, and, moreover, that heavy bombers might be able to deliver such weapons from almost anywhere in the world. This argument gained force after the introduction of in-flight refuelling and of the massive six-engined Convair B-36 bomber, with its range of 13,160 km (8,175 miles), in 1948. Moreover, the success of the *kamikazes* seemed to suggest that carrier task forces would be vulnerable to nuclear bombers or guided missiles (at that time missiles had not been fitted with nuclear warheads).

The *Idaho* (*Mississippi* class), one of the older-generation American battleships, lays down a barrage from its 356 mm (14 in) guns to support the landings at Okinawa on 1 April 1945. During the later phases of the Pacific war the older dreadnoughts were mostly restricted to this 'heavy artillery' role, while newer battleships escorted the fast carrier forces.

CHAPTER 8
MODERN WARSHIPS

When World War II ended in the summer of 1945 some questioned if warships would have any future value. The development of jet-propelled and long-range aircraft and of the atomic bomb raised doubts about the future need for and the survivability of warships. Some military experts believed that submarines could survive in a nuclear war, although it was not known what they could be used for since there might not be any surface ships for them to attack.

The turbojet engine and nuclear energy have profoundly influenced the development of navies in the post-war period, as have two other major developments, automation and electronics. They have not ended the usefulness of warships, but they have changed their nature and even their appearance.

At the end of World War II the United States, Britain, and the Soviet Union were all producing jet-propelled aircraft. The Royal Navy carried out the first carrier tests of jet aircraft in December 1945 with a modified de Havilland Vampire fighter, the F.20. The U.S. Navy soon began operating jet aircraft from flat-tops on a regular basis, spurred on by the Korean War (1950–3) and by the build-up of U.S. naval forces in the Mediterranean and Atlantic to counter the threat of Russian aggression in Europe.

The post-war U.S. carrier force, although considerably reduced from its wartime peak of 28 fleet carriers and 71 small escort carriers, continued to be the main component of the U.S. fleet. Without a hostile fleet to counter, the Navy drew on its war experience of attacking Japanese land targets to develop plans to attack naval installations in the Soviet Union in the event of war. Initially these strikes were to be made with conventional weapons. The U.S. Navy soon developed the first of a series of aircraft that could operate from aircraft carriers and deliver the early nuclear weapons, which weighed five tons. The first carrier-based

aircraft that could carry nuclear weapons was the North American AJ Savage, powered by two piston engines plus a jet booster for high speed over the target.

The first U.S. Navy nuclear-strike aircraft were deployed to the Mediterranean aboard carriers in 1951, followed by similar operations in the Pacific. These aircraft provided the United States with a forward-based nuclear strike force that was totally under American control, and so free of the political problems that might arise if the nuclear weapons or bombers were land-based in friendly countries.

In 1956 the piston-jet Savage was replaced aboard carriers by the twin-jet Douglas A3D Skywarrior strategic bomber; from 1960 the North American A3J Vigilante began joining the fleet, providing U.S. carriers with a supersonic nuclear-strike force. However, the value of these large nuclear-strike aircraft – the A3D weighed about 40,600 kg (40 tons) fully loaded for a mission – was overtaken in the late 1950s by the development of much smaller nuclear weapons that could be carried by fighters and small attack aircraft. Indeed, in 1954 the great designer Ed Heinemann had produced the diminutive, 11,113 kg (10.9-ton) Douglas A4D Skyhawk that could carry a single nuclear weapon against targets several hundred miles from its carrier. (In a war the Skyhawks would not be able to return to the carriers, but would fly to neutral countries or the pilots would bail out at sea, hoping to be picked up by friendly submarines or surface ships.)

Immediately after the war the U.S. Navy had proposed to build large carriers from which these aircraft could operate. The controversy over carrier construction was part of an inter-service rivalry, with the newly established U.S. Air Force calling for a defence policy based almost entirely on long-range strategic bombers. The Navy argued for a more flexible mili-

tary capability, including aircraft carriers. At the height of the debate the first post-war 'super carrier', the 65,000-ton *United States*, was laid down in April 1949, only to be cancelled by the Secretary of Defense two weeks later. The funds appropriated for her went instead to build the huge Convair B-36 strategic bombers.

The Korean War reawakened an appreciation of the importance of warships. Aircraft carriers proved invaluable, sending fighters and ground-attack planes over the Korean peninsula after the Allied airbases had been overrun by the North Korean forces (the American bases in Japan were too far away to provide effective fighter cover). The major U.S. Navy build-up sparked by the war and by the political situation in Europe led to the construction of large carriers that could operate large numbers of the new jet fighters and bombers.

New-generation Carriers

The first new carrier was the USS *Forrestal*, completed in 1955, displacing 75,900 tons fully loaded, and capable of carrying about 90 modern aircraft. The ship's jet fighters weighed some 15,240 kg (15 tons) compared to the 4,570 kg (4.5 tons) of the Grumman F6F Hellcat, the standard U.S. Navy carrier fighter of World War II. During the next 25 years the U.S. Navy built eight of these super-carriers with oil-burning propulsion, plus four even larger carriers with nuclear power. Three of the nuclear ships belong to the *Nimitz* class, at 94,000 tons the largest, most complex, and most expensive warships ever built.

The British Navy, unable to afford new carriers, completed some war-started ships and modernised others to operate jet aircraft such as the Hawker Siddeley Buccaneer, one of the most sophisticated attack aircraft of the early 1960s. This nuclear and conventional strike aircraft had the best night/all-weather performance of its time.

Although British carrier construction lagged, British innovation in carrier technology continued. Notable developments were the steam catapult to launch heavier aircraft and jets, which have a slower rate of initial acceleration than piston aircraft; the mirror landing system to improve the guidance of high-speed aircraft onto the flight deck; and the angled or canted flight deck to permit separate landing and take-off lanes. All these innovations were incorporated into U.S., British, and French carriers (the French Navy building two modern fleet carriers in the early 1960s).

The USS *Nimitz* (1975) and her later sister ships, the *Dwight D. Eisenhower* and *Carl Vinson*, are the second generation of nuclear-powered carriers in the U.S. Navy, following the USS *Enterprise*, which was commissioned in 1961. With an overall length of about 332 m (1,090 ft) they are 3.5 m (12 ft) shorter than the *Enterprise* but at 94,000 tons displace over 4,000 tons more. The *Nimitz*'s engines develop over 280,000 shp and she has a range of up to 1.6 million km (1 million miles) at 30 kts. She carries more than 90 aircraft; the two in the foreground are Grumman F-14 Tomcat multi-role fighters.

A U.S. missile cruiser fires a Talos anti-aircraft missile. During the 1960s and early 1970s the Talos, with a range of more than 160 km (100 miles) and, in some versions, a nuclear warhead, was probably the most powerful anti-aircraft missile in any navy. (The ship is an extensively converted World War II cruiser.)

Guided Missiles

The Russians, helped initially by captured German technology, also developed jet-propelled aircraft, which posed new threats to Western aircraft carriers. In response, the U.S. Navy Bumblebee project, started originally to combat *kamikaze*, produced a 'family' of guided weapons for warships: the Terrier, Talos, and Tartar missiles. These weapons varied in size, so that they could be installed in different sizes of warships, with the larger weapons having greater range – over 160 km (100 miles) in the case of the 1,360 kg (3,000 lb) Talos missile. Some of the Terrier and Talos missiles could be fitted with nuclear warheads designed to destroy formations of approaching enemy aircraft.

These defensive missiles were first installed in existing warships that were rebuilt with missile launchers, magazines, and related missile-control radars and control centres; some or all of the ships' guns were removed to provide space for the missiles. Later, navies began building new missile ships. The U.S. Navy led in anti-aircraft missile development, followed by the British and Soviet navies. Closely related to missile development was the need for more advanced radars to detect targets and guide the missiles, and for computers to predict where the target aircraft (and, later, the missiles) would be when the ship-launched missile could reach an interception point. Although anti-aircraft missiles went to sea in the mid-1950s, the first aircraft to be shot down by ship-launched missiles were North Vietnamese planes destroyed by U.S. warship missiles in the late 1960s. Some of these interceptions were made by Talos missiles over land at distances of about 160 km (100 miles).

While the Bumblebee project led to the postwar anti-aircraft missiles, the German V-1 fly-ing bomb and V-2 (A-4) rocket were the harbingers of sea-based strike missiles. The German Navy had experimented both with short-range rockets, fired from submarines, and with submarines towing V-2 rockets in submersible containers. At the end of the European conflict the U.S. and Soviet armed forces began extensive experiments with V-1 and V-2 missiles. The U.S. Navy fired V-1s from surfaced submarines and other ships, and even launched a 14,225 kg (14-ton) V-2 from an aircraft carrier.

Soon new strike missiles were being developed for both fleets. By the 1950s several guided (cruise) missiles had been produced; some of them, resembling tiny unmanned aircraft, could be fired from submarines on the surface or from surface ships. They were propelled by jet and rocket engines and, unlike ballistic missiles that follow bullet-like trajectories, had a variable flight path and could be guided to strike moving targets.

The U.S. Navy's Regulus guided missile of this era could deliver an atomic bomb against land targets up to 925 km (575 miles) distant. Two submarines were converted to fire the Regulus and several new ones were built for that purpose, including one with nuclear propulsion. Some of these submarines were continuously on patrol off the Soviet Siberian coast from 1960 to 1964 as part of the U.S. strategic-deterrence force. The construction of further Regulus submarines and development of improved cruise missiles halted abruptly when the U.S. Navy embarked on the Polaris submarine-launched ballistic missile. The Soviet Navy continued the development of cruise missiles as well as ballistic missiles.

After the war Josef Stalin, the Soviet dictator, had given high priority to building a large, conventional fleet – cruisers, destroyers, and submarines, with battlecruisers and aircraft carriers being planned. Stalin died in March 1953 and his successors halted the naval build-up. Large ships, they felt, were too expensive and too vulnerable to Western aircraft. Instead, the new Russian leaders decided to concentrate on a coastal-defence navy of submarines, small surface craft, and land-based bombers, armed with conventional weapons and with anti-ship missiles. Admiral Sergei G. Gorshkov was appointed head of the Soviet Navy in January 1956 to supervise the dismantling of the older battleships and cruisers and the building of this coastal-defence force. By the late 1950s the Russians were building large numbers of submarines, surface ships, and aircraft to attack Western warships if they ventured near the Soviet Union. (Some of the submarines and surface ships were also being armed with missiles to attack the United States, as we shall see in a moment.)

Cruise missiles, some large and with ranges almost as great as that of the Regulus, were installed in Soviet coastal missile boats, surface ships, and submarines, and were carried by land-based bombers such as the Tupolev Tu-16 'Badger'. Although originally developed for attacks against land targets, missiles evolved into primarily anti-ship weapons. Their principal targets were the American, British, and French aircraft carriers, which the Russians feared would send nuclear bombers against their homeland in time of war.

A related development of the 1960s was the Soviet Union's attempt to influence Third World countries by providing some of them with anti-ship missiles. Egypt and Indonesia were especially favoured with naval weapons, and Western world naval leaders were shocked when, on 21 October 1967, Egyptian 75-ton *Komar*-class missile boats in harbour sank the Israeli destroyer *Elath* with Styx missiles. Although the *Elath*, a former British 'Z'-class ship, was 23 years old, she was still a capable warship. The *Elath* was the first warship to be sunk by missiles fired by another ship. Four years later the Styx-armed Indian Navy *Osa*-class

missile boats carried out extensive missile strikes against the Pakistani fleet, sinking several warships and merchant vessels.

Navies clashed for the first time in missile-versus-missile battles during the Yom Kippur war of 1973. After the *Elath* loss the Israelis had given up all large ships and concentrated on a fleet of small missile ships (firing the Israeli-developed Gabriel missile) and submarines. In a series of dramatic battles in 1973, Israeli missile boats destroyed 13 Egyptian and Syrian missile boats armed with Styx missiles without loss or damage to themselves.

The Israeli success showed that a combination of tactics and countermeasures, if astutely employed, could negate the threat of the anti-ship missile. Countermeasures could include attempting to shoot down 'incoming' missiles with guns or defensive missiles; reducing the radar and heat (infrared) 'signatures' of a ship (on which missiles can be 'homed'); using 'chaff' – thin strips of metal foil fired into the air – to confuse missile guidance; and electronic jamming of enemy radars.

Weapon begets counter-weapon, and the *Elath* sinking had caused Western navies to develop countermeasures of all kinds against the anti-ship missile, and to develop their own anti-ship missiles. Clearly, the best way to counter the threat of an enemy missile is to sink or incapacitate the launching ship before it fires. This may well be possible in the case of enemy surface ships, but dealing with submarine missile launchers has become exceedingly difficult.

Upper Naval forces depend for their operational range and flexibility on a fleet of supply vessels. Even nuclear-powered carriers need to be supplied regularly with fuel for their aircraft and food and other material for their crews. Here a U.S. Navy oiler (left) transfers fuel and supplies to a carrier underway, while a Boeing Vertol CH-47 helicopter shuttles missiles.

Lower An Egyptian Navy Russian-built *Osa II*-class missile boat at sea. The boat displaces 210 tons, is 39 m (128 ft) long, and is capable of 32 kts. It is armed with four Styx SSM (surface-to-surface missiles), with a range of 48 km (30 miles), and four 30 mm guns.

Submarines

At the end of World War II German submarine technology and several submarines passed into Allied hands. New submarines were built in the United States and Soviet Union based on the German Type XXI, which were capable of making over 16 knots underwater for an hour and had a submerged endurance of several days at low speeds. Even though some surface warships could steam at double that speed, the advanced submarine was immune to rough weather that would slow the surface ship, and when going slow the virtually silent electric motors of the submarine made her almost undetectable to enemy ASW vessels.

But submarines were still submersibles: although they could remain underwater for days on end, eventually they had to come near the surface so that their schnorkel breathing tube could draw in air to enable their diesel engines to recharge the batteries which powered their electric motors. American scientists and engineers were considering the potential of nuclear energy to power machinery even as they were developing the atomic bomb. After the war development of submarine nuclear propulsion was eventually directed by Hyman G. Rickover, a naval engineer. The first nuclear vehicle ever built was the USS *Nautilus*, a combat submarine completed early in 1955. She was powered by a nuclear reactor that could drive her under water at speeds of about 25 knots and could remain submerged for virtually unlimited periods. On her original nuclear 'fueling' *Nautilus* travelled more than 100,000 km (62,000 miles) during a two-year period, almost all of that distance submerged. Subsequently, reactor-fuel cores have permitted a high-speed submarine endurance of several hundred thousand miles before refuelling is necessary.

The first Soviet nuclear-powered submarine, given the NATO codename 'November' class, entered service in 1959. British and French nuclear undersea craft soon followed. Nuclear propulsion has provided the long-sought independence of the surface atmosphere for the submarine; its turbines are driven by steam raised not by air-breathing oil engines but by a reactor that generates heat by the process of nuclear fission – a process that does not require the presence of oxygen. The oxygen required for the submarine's crew is extracted from sea water by special equipment.

Nuclear submarines are expensive to build, their crews must be carefully selected and extensively trained, and their engines are much noisier (and hence more easily detectable) than electric motors. But their virtually unlimited high-speed underwater endurance has made nuclear submarines a vital component of the world's major navies.

The marriage of the missile and the nuclear submarine occurred in the U.S. and Soviet fleets almost at the same time. One U.S. nuclear submarine was fitted to fire the Regulus cruise missile before that programme was halted, while the Russians have continued to build specialised cruise-missile submarines. Later, the U.S. Navy developed two anti-ship missiles that could be fired from standard, 538 mm (21 in) torpedo tubes: the Harpoon, with a range of about 97 km (60 miles), and the Tomahawk, with a range some 10 times greater.

ACTIVE NUCLEAR-PROPELLED SHIPS, January 1980

	USA	UK	France	USSR
Attack submarines	77	10	–	85
Strategic missile submarines	41	4	5	72
Aircraft carriers	3	–	–	–
Missile carriers	8	–	–	1
Icebreakers	–	–	–	3
Research submarines	1	–	–	–

All these countries are building more nuclear submarines; the Soviet Union also has nuclear carriers and cruisers under construction, while France is building a small nuclear carrier. In addition, Japan has a nuclear-propelled research ship. Two U.S. and one Soviet nuclear submarines have been lost at sea; several others are no longer in service.

Main picture A Lockheed S-3A Viking and, behind it, a Grumman EA-6B Prowler aboard the carrier *John F. Kennedy*. Both aircraft are four-seaters and bristle with electronic systems. The Viking is an anti-submarine aircraft, carrying torpedoes, bombs, or mines internally and bombs, missiles, or extra fuel tanks on wing pods. The Prowler is an electronic countermeasures (ECM) aircraft used for jamming enemy electronic devices.

Inset A U.S. Navy Sikorsky SH-3 Sea King lowers an ASW sonar into the sea. The helicopter can also release expendable sonobuoys to listen for submarines. It has radar for detecting schnorkel tubes, and it is armed with acoustic-homing torpedoes.

Nuclear Missiles

More significant has been the development of submarine-launched ballistic missiles (SLBM) for strategic attack against an enemy's homeland. The Soviet Navy put the first SLBMs to sea in the late 1950s. These early strategic missiles were of short range – about 485 km (300 miles) – with a nuclear warhead, and were carried in both diesel-electric and nuclear submarines. The United States, spurred to action in the strategic-weapons field by the Soviet Sputnik satellites (1957–8) and strategic-missile tests, initiated the top-priority Polaris Programme.

The early Soviet strategic missiles had liquid fuels. American technology provided more-stable solid propellants that were better suited for shipboard use. In record time the U.S. Navy developed and put to sea the 1,950 km (1,200-mile) range Polaris A-1 SLBM, the nuclear-propelled submarine USS *George Washington* beginning a 60-day 'deterrent patrol' late in 1960. During the next few years the United States put 40 additional Polaris submarines to sea, each carrying 16 nuclear-tipped missiles. The initial 1,950 km range was soon extended to 2,415 km (1,500 miles) and then to 4,025 km (2,500 miles). Further, the submarines' design permitted later refitting of the Poseidon SLBM, with slightly shorter range, but with each

missile carrying some 10 nuclear warheads that could be dispersed over an area of several hundred square kilometres.

Another innovation of the Polaris submarines was the 'blue-and-gold' crew system (the term refers to the U.S. Navy's traditional colours). Under this system each submarine has two full crews of about 140 men each. While one crew is at sea for a two-month underwater cruise, the other is ashore on leave or in training. Then, when the submarine returns to port for replenishment, the crews switch and the alternate crew takes the submarine to sea for the next two-month cruise. This scheme permits about half of the 41 Polaris-Poseidon submarines to be at sea at any given time.

Polaris missiles with British-made nuclear warheads are also used in the Royal Navy's four SLBM submarines of the *Resolution* class. The French Navy, without the benefit of American technology, developed its own nuclear-power plants and submarine-launched missiles, and has constructed five strategic-missile submarines of the *Le Redoutable* class.

In some respects the most dramatic SLBM submarine developments have been Russian. In 1967, when the Soviet Union was developing the world's largest land-based intercontinental ballistic missile (ICBM) force, the Soviet Navy launched the first 'Yankee'-class submarine, nuclear propelled and with 16 SS-N-6 missiles of 2,100 km (1,300-mile) range. Thirty-four 'Yankees' were built, followed by some 30 of the larger 'Delta' class, carrying 12 or (in later submarines) 16 missiles. The SLBMs of the 'Delta' class have a range of more than 6,450 km (4,000 miles) and carry multiple warheads. Obviously, all of Europe is within range of even the older Soviet missile submarines. The giant 'Delta'-class submarines, displacing more than 10,000 tons – the size of a cruiser – can launch missiles against most major American cities without even leaving their home ports on the Soviet Arctic and Siberian coasts.

During the 1980s the U.S. Navy will take delivery of a series of still larger submarines, the 18,700-ton giants of the *Ohio* class, each with 24 Trident missiles with a range of some 6,450 km (4,000 miles) and with multiple warheads. But the size of these submarines, and the relatively few that will probably be built to provide the sea-based portion of American strategic deterrence, have raised questions about the Trident's vulnerability to future Soviet anti-submarine measures.

Anti-submarine warfare (ASW) was mainly an Anglo-American concern during the two world wars. After World War II, recognizing the potential threat of a Soviet submarine force based on German technology, the United States and other NATO navies made enormous investments in ASW forces: anti-submarine ships, aircraft, airships (blimps), and hunter-killer submarines were developed, as well as sea-floor sound-surveillance systems (SOSUS). The SOSUS is a network of underwater cables and listening devices in the Atlantic and Pacific, as well as in some regional areas, that try to detect Soviet submarines at sea, reporting their positions to shore stations which, in turn, direct ASW aircraft and submarines.

At the same time, there have been major improvements in the ASW performance of surface ships and submarines, including long-range sonars, rockets that can propel an anti-submarine torpedo or a nuclear depth charge several miles from the launching ship, small helicopters carried aboard ship, expendable sonobuoys that are dropped at sea to detect submarines and radio their information to aircraft, and electronic interception devices that can locate a submarine when it transmits a radio message. The Soviet Navy began major ASW efforts in the early 1960s after the U.S. Polaris submarines first went to sea. Since then the Soviet Union has made a massive investment in anti-submarine forces.

Perhaps the most surprising naval development since World War II has been the Soviet Union's development of major ocean-going naval forces combining both submarines and surface ships. The most startling submarine development has been the nuclear-powered 'Alpha' class. These submarines were first observed about 1970, but they had a long trial period and apparently were extensively modified before the design was adopted for series production. The 'Alpha' is credited with a submerged speed of over 40 knots and an operating depth of more than 610 m (2,000 ft) – both features being superior to those of any NATO submarine at present at sea.

Another dramatic Soviet naval programme has been the aircraft carrier. For many years the Russians believed the carrier to be obsolete, but in about 1970 they decided that such ships were justified and in 1977 the first ship of the *Kiev* class was completed. Displacing about 40,000 tons, the *Kiev* operates some 35 helicopters and vertical/short-take-off-and-landing (V/STOL) aircraft and has a considerable battery of guns and missiles for use against air, surface, and underwater targets. The *Kiev*-class carriers are the largest warships yet built in the Soviet Union. This class of four ships will probably be followed by a still larger carrier, displacing perhaps 50–60,000 tons and having nuclear propulsion. At the same time, the Soviet Navy is building several missile cruiser classes. One of these, the giant *Kirov*, displacing about 30,000 tons and with nuclear propulsion, was completed in 1979 and is the largest warship other than an aircraft carrier to be built by any nation since World War II.

Soviet nuclear submarines.

Top One of the 'Echo'-class (1963–7), of 6,000 tons, raises four of her eight 'Shaddock' missile tubes.

Middle A 'Yankee'-class (1967–75) submarine, similar to the American Polaris type, of 9,000 tons, and armed with 16 nuclear missiles.

Bottom A 'Delta'-class (1973 onwards), of about 10,000 tons, capable of 30 kts submerged. It is armed with 12 or 16 nuclear missiles with a range of over 7,365 km (4,575 miles) – the farthest-reaching ship-borne missiles of their generation.

Main picture The *Minsk*, a sister ship of the *Kiev* (1976), which was the Soviet Navy's first true aircraft carrier; a third carrier of this class has been completed and a fourth is being built. The *Minsk* displaces about 40,000 tons, is 285 m (935 ft) long, and can make 30 kts. She carries over 30 ASW helicopters, such as the Kamov Ka-25 'Hormone', and V/STOL fixed-wing attack aircraft. She is armed with SSM and SAM launchers and also four 76 mm (3 in) guns.

The Future

It is difficult to compare the qualities of rival naval technologies except in the heat of battle – when other elements, such as tactics, training, and discipline, might also contribute decisively to the outcome. The U.S. and Soviet navies are far larger and more advanced than any other, and this discrepancy in size and sophistication is increasing. In the future, as in the past, naval superiority will depend fundamentally on budgets and appropriations. It is clear that the crude equation, sometimes propounded in the West, of NATO quality versus Soviet quantity is no longer valid. As we enter the 1980s the mantle of world naval leadership in several respects is passing to the Soviet Union. If Western technology still has the edge, the Soviet Navy has shown itself able to put highly advanced hardware – both ships and missile systems – to sea more quickly than the NATO powers.

Developments in ship design and means of propulsion, in guidance systems, in methods of communication and interdiction, have trans-formed the major navies since World War II. Most such advances have been devoted to the end sought by navies of the past: command, or at least dominance, of the sea. But the coming of the nuclear-powered submarine armed with SLBMs with thermonuclear warheads has transformed not merely the practice of the naval arts but war itself. SLBMs are pointed not at enemy warships but at the land. Like land-based IABMs they are capable of annihilating whole cities and their populations in the heartlands of distant continents; unlike ICBMs they are launched from moving vehicles that are exceptionally difficult to locate and destroy. If successfully used in war they would render the formidable fighting power of modern surface vessels and naval aircraft not merely obsolete but irrelevant. It is the further development of these submarines and their weapons and, even more urgent, the development of authentically effective systems to counter them, that is likely to dominate the evolution of the world's major navies in the future.

Inset HMS *Invincible*, first
of Britain's through-deck
anti-submarine cruisers, was
completed in 1980. She
has a full-load displacement
of 19,500 tons and is 193 m
(632 ft) long. Her gas-
turbine engines deliver
110,000 shp, and give her a
range of about 8,000 km
(5,000 miles) and a speed of
about 28 kts. She operates
15 Westland Sea King HAS.1
helicopters and British
Aerospace Sea Harrier FRS.1
V/STOL aircraft, and is armed
with Sea Dart SAM. Note the
upward-sloping forward end
of the flight deck, designed
to assist take off of the Sea
Harrier in the STOL mode.

INDEX

ACKNOWLEDGMENTS

The publishers thank the following organizations and individuals for their permission to reproduce the photographs in this book:

David Brown Gear Industries Ltd 2–3; Jean-Loup Charmet 39 above; Richard Cooke endpapers, 68–69, 75; Ehrlich Tweedy Archive 32 inset, 39 centre, 49 below right; Robert Hunt Library 37, 46–47; Imperial War Museum 19 above right, 26, 27, 28 centre and below left, 29, 30–31, 34 above left, 36, 48, 49 above right; Imperial War Museum/Ehrlich Tweedy Archive 35, 38; John MacClancy 9, 25, 67; Ministry of Defence/Royal Navy 79 inset; National Maritime Museum 1; National Maritime Museum/Ehrlich Tweedy Archive 8, 12–13, 14–15, 18, 19 below, 20–21, 32–33

The following pictures are kindly supplied by the author:

6–7, 17, 23, 29, 43 inset, 45, 50–51, 52, 56 above, 61, 62, 70, 73 below, 75 inset, 76, 77; (Imperial War Museum) 28 above left, 34 below left, 39 below; (U.S. Army) 57; (U.S. Bureau of Ships) 34 above right; (U.S. Navy Department) 4–5, 16, 40–41, 43, 53, 54–55, 56 below, 57, 58–59, 64 and inset, 65, 66, 71, 72, 73 above, 74, 76 inset, 78–79; (U.S. Naval Institute) 22